GIRL CEO

Priceless advice from trailblazing women

By RONNIE COHEN and KATHERINE ELLISON

Illustrated by GEORGIA RUCKER

downtown bookworks

downtown bookworks

Downtown Bookworks Inc.
265 Canal Street, New York, NY 10013
www.downtownbookworks.com

Copyright © 2018 Downtown Bookworks Inc.
Designed and illustrated by Georgia Rucker
Printed in China, March 2019
10 9 8 7 6 5 4 3 2

CONTENTS

- 6 **Foreword**
- 8 **Introduction**
- 12 **Noa Mintz** | Founder of Nannies by Noa
Make the Most of Your Kind of Smarts
- 16 **Haile Thomas** | Founder and CEO of The HAPPY Organization
Choose a Business Close to Your Heart
- 20 **Diane von Furstenberg** | Fashion designer, founder and co-chairman of DVF
Find Your Signature
- 24 **Bridget Hilton** | Founder of LSTN Sound Co.
Incorporate a Cause
- 28 **Muriel "Mickie" Siebert** | First woman to own a seat on the New York Stock Exchange, CEO of Muriel Siebert & Co.
Rock the Boat
- 32 **Katrina Lake** | Founder and CEO of Stitch Fix
Find an Unmet Need and Fill It
- 36 **Judy Faulkner** | Founder and CEO of Epic Systems
Nerds Rule
- 40 **Ursula Burns** | Former CEO of Xerox
Embrace STEM
- 43 **Tavi Gevinson** | Founder and editor-in-chief of *Rookie*
Find Your Voice
- 46 **Mariam Naficy** | Founder and CEO of Minted
Let the Customer Choose and Stay Fresh Forever
- 50 **Oprah Winfrey** | Media mogul, chairman and CEO of OWN: Oprah Winfrey Network
Be Willing to Change

53 **Reese Witherspoon** | Producer, founder of Hello Sunshine
Leverage Success

56 **Josephine Cochrane** | Inventor
Timing Is Everything

60 **Debbie Sterling** | Founder and CEO of GoldieBlox
Kick-Start Your Dream

64 **Lilly Singh** | Comedian, YouTube star
Be Your Own Superhero

68 **Mikaila Ulmer** | Founder of Me & the Bees Lemonade
You're Never Too Young to Start a Business

72 **Estée Lauder** | Founder of Estée Lauder Companies
Reward Your Customers

76 **Rachel Zietz** | Founder and CEO of Gladiator Lacrosse
Be the Brand

80 **Ayanna Howard** | Founder and CTO of Zyrobotics
Do Good to Do Well

83 **Katharine Graham** | Former CEO and publisher of *The Washington Post*
Excellence Leads to Success

86 **Julie Rice & Elizabeth Cutler** | Co-founders of SoulCycle
Make It Fun

90 **Francesca Kennedy** | Founder and CEO of Ix Style
Build a Network

94 **Rosanna Pansino** | Baker, YouTube star
Be Choosy

97 **Pleasant Rowland** | Founder of Pleasant Company and creator of the American Girl empire
Market Directly to Your Customers

100 **Jessica Alba** | Founder of The Honest Company
Learn on the Job

104 **Limor Fried** | Founder and CEO of Adafruit Industries
Do It Yourself

108 **Venus Williams** | Tennis champion, founder and CEO of EleVen by Venus
Know Your Customers

112 **Anne Wojcicki** | Co-founder and CEO of 23andMe
Setbacks Are Opportunities to Learn

116 **J.K. Rowling** | Author and creator of the Harry Potter empire
Keep Control of Your Brand

120 **Mary Barra** | Chairman and CEO of General Motors
Do the Right Thing

124 **Madam C.J. Walker** | Founder of Madam C.J. Walker Manufacturing Company
Grow a Grassroots Sales Force

128 **Heidi Ganahl** | Founder of Camp Bow Wow
Build a Franchise

132 **Linda Alvarado** | President and CEO of Alvarado Construction
Redefine Women's Work

136 **Taylor Swift** | Singer, songwriter
Know Your Value

140 **Sheryl Sandberg** | COO of Facebook and founder of LeanIn.Org
Give It All You've Got

144 **Kimberly Bryant** | Founder and executive director of Black Girls Code
Be a Role Model

148 **Joy Mangano** | Inventor, founder and president of Ingenious Designs
Turn No into Yes

152 **Alice Waters** | Founder, owner, and executive chef of Chez Panisse restaurant
Envision, Empower, Delegate

156 **Prerna Gupta** | Founder and CEO of Hooked
Dare to Be Different

160 **Learn More!**

FOREWORD

If you are curious about how other women have succeeded in business, you are probably thinking about how you will make your mark in the world. This could be the first sign of your ambition, and I hope you will embrace it.

When I first thought about launching a fashion company, there were many obstacles. I had to raise money. I had to convince people that it made sense to launch with a retail store and an e-commerce site. People told me that no one would buy online. But I believed in what I was doing. I knew what was missing from my closet, and I thought other women might be missing similar things. So I kept making phone calls and sharing my ideas. I assembled a team of amazing people who could help me turn my concept into a collection, and we all worked incredibly hard. We knew we were onto something when we almost sold through our inventory on the first day. Ambition and perseverance turned out to be good things.

There is more to my story. I started my company because I wanted to start a foundation for women. The Tory Burch Foundation empowers women entrepreneurs by providing affordable loans, business education, mentorship, and a fellowship program. As you think about your future, I hope you will also think about ways that you can give back from the outset.

There are many different measures of success, but to achieve any of them, it is important to believe in yourself and your ideas. Dream big and embrace your ambition!

—TORY BURCH
Founder of Tory Burch Foundation
Chairman, CEO, and designer of Tory Burch

INTRODUCTION

What do you want to be when you grow up? As the 40 women in this book demonstrate, your choices are limitless. Maybe you want to program robots to help kids with disabilities. Or create your own TV network. Or lead a major manufacturing company. Or start a doggy daycare franchise. Or be the first woman to—fill in the blank.

The world needs more women with big dreams. So let your imagination fly!

Haile Thomas and Rachel Zietz, two young women profiled in the book, had a clear idea about what they wanted to do when they were just 12 years old. Haile channeled her concern over her father's diabetes diagnosis into a nonprofit organization. Rachel turned her love of lacrosse into a business. Other women in the book discovered their passion when they were well into their adult years. There's no rush to decide as long as you enjoy the adventure of discovery. Then, whatever you choose, we hope you'll wake up every morning, or at least most mornings, looking forward to going to work.

We also hope the women described in these pages inspire you on your journey, wherever it leads. Many of the women are entrepreneurs, which means they came up with an original idea for a company and then created it. Some of them run their own businesses as chief executive officers, or CEOs. Still others have "disrupted" their industries by changing the rules to their advantage.

We chose a diverse group of women, born as early as 1839 and as recently as 2004. They come from varied racial, ethnic, and economic backgrounds. Oprah Winfrey's family was so poor when she was growing up in Mississippi that she wore dresses sewn from potato sacks. Joy Mangano was struggling to pay her electric bill and support her three young children when she invented her Miracle Mop. At the other extreme, Diane von Furstenberg benefited from the financial support and social ties of her husband, a wealthy prince, when she introduced her clothing line.

Most of the women earned college degrees. Four went on to earn advanced degrees in business administration. A few attended college on scholarships and financial aid. Not all completed college. LSTN founder Bridget Hilton went straight from high school to work in the music industry.

Some came to this country as immigrants or were born to immigrants. Because Hooked founder Prerna Gupta and YouTube star Lilly Singh, both children of immigrants, experienced the world as outsiders, they developed the kind of dogged determination entrepreneurs need to succeed.

Many of the women blazed new trails. Mary Barra worked her way up from GM's factory floor to become the first woman CEO of a major automaker. Ursula Burns was the first African-American woman to lead a Fortune 500 company. Muriel Siebert was the first woman to own a seat on the New York Stock Exchange. Katharine Graham was the first woman publisher of a major American newspaper. Judy Faulkner started a medical software company in 1979, when very few women worked in technology.

Backed by their economic power, several of these entrepreneurs have revolutionized aspects of their industries. Pop star Taylor Swift has found new ways for musicians to control how their concert tickets are sold. Sheryl Sandberg, Facebook's chief operating officer, has inspired women to "lean in" and power their way to the top of corporations. By teaching African-American girls to program computers, Kimberly Bryant, founder of Black Girls Code, intends to transform the face of the technology industry.

Each woman's journey offers a different lesson. But we were struck by how much these leaders had in common.

Taking risks—an important part of an entrepreneur's job—was a recurring theme. Rosanna Pansino invested her life's savings to make her wildly popular Nerdy Nummies YouTube videos. Francesca Kennedy quit her high-paying job at a financial-services firm to sell sandals and provide jobs and clean drinking water in Guatemala.

Of course, sometimes taking risks can be dangerous. That's just the point. Yet several women insisted that they learned more from failing than from succeeding. They stressed how important it was to pick themselves up after making a mistake. "I've learned that failure is just a step towards greatness," said Heidi Ganahl, founder of Camp Bow Wow. "Don't fear it, embrace it."

When faced with challenges, many women turned to their families. Noa Mintz's father helped her launch a website and register her babysitter service as a business. Alice Waters' parents mortgaged their house so she could start her influential restaurant. Some women gave special credit to their mothers for encouraging them. The "fighter mentality" that Anne Wojcicki learned from her mother helped her endure a year when she almost lost control of her company, 23andMe.

Several women incorporated philanthropy into their companies after realizing customers were demanding products that pair charity with merchandise. Francesca Kennedy, Bridget Hilton, and Mikaila Ulmer knit social missions into the core of their businesses.

We wrote *Girl CEO* against the backdrop of a growing, social-media-driven movement to empower women. The #MeToo and #TimesUp campaigns have exposed and challenged male harassment of women in the workplace. Regardless of how women's opportunities change in the future, one thing will remain the same. It will continue to be up to every one of us to put in the effort and take the risks required to find and keep work that's fulfilling—and pays the bills. The days of women being kept out of corporate boardrooms and top leadership roles are over—and good riddance, right? As these 40 women show, if you find your passion and work hard, the sky's the limit. Write your own story.

— RONNIE COHEN AND KATHERINE ELLISON

Noa Mintz

MAKE THE MOST OF **YOUR KIND** OF SMARTS

Noa Mintz was having a hard time in grade school. She couldn't keep up with her classes. She wasn't athletic or popular. And sometimes she even felt dissed by her nanny, who seemed to prefer spending time with Noa's baby sister.

Other girls might have been permanently discouraged. But Mintz bounced back to turn those challenges into a phenomenal business success.

At the age of 12, she created a new company, called Nannies by Noa, dedicated to improving relationships between babysitters and the children they care for. "I think my main secret was my obsession with quality," she said. "I wasn't doing it for the money. I didn't need to pay my bills. I had a mission."

Her first mission was to find a better match for herself. Her mother agreed to interview a half-dozen candidates, so Noa scouted job-applicant sites, screening scores of possibilities to come up with the most promising six. *Score!* She got a babysitter who wasn't only interested in babies.

She went on to find the perfect "manny" (that's a male nanny) for a family friend whose son she had played with. "I knew what he was like, so it was easier to find someone I knew he'd get along with," she said. She was right: the family adored their new sitter.

As Noa began to ramp up her business, she stayed up late into the night, studying other nanny agencies to see what they were doing right and wrong. She chose a logo, designed her own website, and with help from her father registered as an LLC, or limited liability company. (An LLC is one type of business structure. The type of business structure you choose affects things like taxes and whether you are personally responsible if your business is ever sued.) Then she began screening and interviewing hundreds of job applicants, initially charging $100 for a match.

> **"THERE IS SOMETHING PROFOUNDLY SATISFYING ABOUT TAKING A CREATIVE IDEA AND TURNING IT INTO A REALITY."**

As her business caught on, Noa felt she'd found her calling. "I started not to mind that I would probably never get a straight-A report card," she said. "Getting someone a job—improving a life—that felt so much more satisfying!"

There's a double-edged secret to Noa's success. In fourth grade, she was diagnosed with attention deficit hyperactivity disorder, or ADHD. Some of the common symptoms are distraction and forgetfulness. Yet many people with ADHD also have higher-than-average intuition, creativity, and enthusiasm for the pursuits they choose. That's one reason why the disorder is so common among entrepreneurs.

"I'm a poster child for ADHD," Noa said. "Everyone is wired differently, and for me, there was a big advantage in learning how I was wired very early, so I could start doing something about it."

She was determined to make the most of her natural talents, including her skill at understanding people's feelings. That compassion helped Noa in her interviews with nannies and potential employers. In 45-minute sessions, followed by social media screenings and reference checks, she figured out families' needs and gauged nannies' enthusiasm and commitment—or lack thereof. "People appreciated that I cared in a different way, that I had the mindset of still being an age where I needed a nanny myself—so I understood what other kids needed," she explained.

Pretty soon, Nannies by Noa was serving hundreds of families, with revenues in the hundreds of thousands of dollars.

"Before that, I hadn't felt very valued, so I focused on what other kids were doing," Noa said. "But now I had my own thing, where there was always something new. One day I'd be working on legal stuff, another day I'd be interviewing or managing people. It was great!"

She was working a full 40-hour workweek—and she still had to get through high school. Her parents insisted she get some help to reduce the workload, so Noa hired a former nanny as her first CEO. Among other things, that gave her the time she needed to ace her college applications, winning a place at Brown University, a top-ranked Ivy League school.

Now, as a freshman in college, she still isn't sure what she'll choose for a major, or how much time she'll be able to dedicate to Nannies by Noa. She predicts one thing with confidence, however. "Maybe I'll be a social entrepreneur, or maybe I'll be a tech entrepreneur," she said. "But whatever I do, I'll always be an entrepreneur."

WHAT IS A CEO?

The CEO, or chief executive officer, is the top position at a company. The duties of a CEO can be different depending on the business. But, in general, the CEO will be the company's main decision-maker, responsible for helping the company reach its goals. Often a CEO is the face of the company, too. She will explain what the company is doing and provide leadership for the employees. At a start-up (a newly established business), the CEO may be in charge of nearly everything, from raising money to creating products and making sales.

Haile Thomas

CHOOSE A BUSINESS CLOSE TO YOUR **HEART**

Haile Thomas felt her world shift in 2009 when she was 8 years old. Her family was driving home after a doctor had diagnosed her father with type 2 diabetes. Her mother was reading off a list of possible side effects from the medicine the doctor prescribed: rashes, diarrhea, and internal bleeding. Worse, the diabetes itself could blind Haile's 41-year-old father. It could even kill him.

Haile's mother immediately began to change the family's diet. They had been eating dishes like curry goat and oxtail from Jamaica, Haile's parents' home country. The menu was heavy on meat, rich sauces, and white rice and light on fruits and vegetables. With Haile's help, her mother began cooking tasty, organic, plant-based food. Haile started reading about nutrition and watching food documentaries. At her suggestion, the family ultimately switched to a vegan diet.

Haile's father never took the prescribed medication. Within a year, he no longer had diabetes. "We were definitely really scared," Haile said. "But I think being so scared kind of forced us into action. We found out that food could be the cause and definitely the cure as well."

The short-lived diabetes diagnosis started Haile on a crusade. She'd see a friend snacking on potato chips and warn: "Put down the potato chips, or you're going to die." Soon she learned that trying to scare people didn't work. She shifted to a positive approach and began educating her classmates about healthier food choices in the encouraging way her mother had used with her. Then her peers welcomed her message, and she began spreading it.

"I was confused why none of my classmates knew about factory farming or read food labels. I was confused why this wasn't a mandatory thing in schools," she said. She took a seat on the youth advisory board for the Alliance for a Healthier Generation. The group works to combat childhood obesity.

Then, when she was only 12 years old, Haile started HAPPY. The acronym stands for Healthy Active Positive Purposeful Youth. It's a nonprofit organization that offers cooking and nutrition classes and workshops in schools and camps for kids around the world, especially in poor U.S. neighborhoods. The organization also provides HAPPY Kits to elementary schools and community groups. The kits include videos with cooking lessons, games, quizzes, and recipes. Haile is HAPPY's CEO.

By 2018, Haile had personally taught 15,000 kids. During a workshop at an elementary school, she measured out sugar to show the students how much of it was in their cereal. "The point of this is not to scare you, but it really shows us how weird our food can be," she told the enthusiastic students.

"We really just want to be sure that every kid has the opportunity to know how to make a healthy

WHAT IS A NONPROFIT?

Profit is the money a business makes after all the costs and expenses are paid. (If you made $20 selling lemonade, but spent $8 on lemons, sugar, cups, and signs, then your profit would be $12.) Most companies aim to make as much profit as possible.

Nonprofits are different. They have a mission to help others in some way. They may make money, but that isn't the main goal. And the money they earn goes back into the organization so it can help more people. One of the main ways that nonprofits earn money is through fundraising. The employees of a nonprofit ask people for donations. They also apply for grants, which are donations from institutions or the government.

choice . . . So we go over reading food labels, researching ingredients, and really understanding serving sizes," Haile said. "We try to let kids know you really want to go to farmers' markets and eat organic and not support these other companies that sell you poison."

Haile has worked with leaders of the healthy food movement, including Michelle Obama and Chelsea Clinton. "She has helped more people than she will ever know be healthy, and she's inspired so many people, including me," Clinton said of Haile.

Haile makes running a nonprofit look easy. But it can present challenges. On top of the other work that CEOs must do, nonprofit executives have to raise money, a time-consuming and sometimes frustrating chore. A friend once advised Haile not to let the need to raise money for her organization kill her love for her mission. "With that passion and persistence, miracles can happen," Haile said.

She's thrilled when kids who arrive at her summer camp workshops with candy and soda in their lunch boxes return home determined to replace sugary snacks and drinks with healthier choices.

"I am truly able to see lives transform right in front of me, and it's just that one moment where a kid realizes that they can do better for themselves and their families that is so important to me," Haile said. "That's exactly what helped my dad get better."

> **"SO MANY TIMES WE LOOK OUTWARDLY FOR ACCEPTANCE OR VALIDATION, AND I THINK IT TAKES A CERTAIN AMOUNT OF STRENGTH AND BOLDNESS TO SAY, 'YOU KNOW WHAT, I AM GOING TO BELIEVE IN MYSELF.'"**

Diane von Furstenberg

FIND **YOUR** SIGNATURE

Diane von Furstenberg designed a dress she'd be comfortable wearing to work, to dinner, or to a party. And, to her surprise, that dress became a must-have for millions of women for decades.

"I created the wrap dress, but in a sense, it's the wrap dress that created me," she said. "The dress became the vehicle of becoming confident—not just for me, but for a generation, many generations, of women. So the dress decided to have a life on its own."

Von Furstenberg first showed the wrap dress in 1974, when women were starting to enter the workforce in greater numbers. It never occurred to her that a simple dress made of cotton jersey that wraps around like a bathrobe and ties at the waist would become an iconic piece of clothing and a cultural phenomenon worthy of a museum exhibit. "I had no idea that one day it would hang in the Smithsonian Institution," she wrote in her autobiography *Diane: A Signature Life*. "I just thought it was a good dress."

Diana Vreeland, the editor in chief of *Vogue*, the fashion world's most influential magazine at the time, recognized something more. In 1970, von Furstenberg brought a Louis Vuitton suitcase filled with a dozen dresses in three styles to Vreeland's office. Gesturing with red-painted fingernails, the editor declared the clothes "absolutely smashing." Vreeland's endorsement launched the 23-year-old's career.

To announce the opening of her showroom in 1972, von Furstenberg planned to take out an ad in *Women's Wear Daily*, a magazine for people who worked in the fashion industry. But she had no advertising agency, no model, and no photographer. So she asked a friend to snap a picture of her sitting on a white cube in one of her favorite shirtdresses. She looked at the black-and-white photo, decided it needed something, picked up a pen, and scribbled on the cube: "Feel like a woman, wear a dress! Diane von Furstenberg."

"That handwritten copy line and my signature in the first ad I created would appear on every dress tag for the next decade and become my registered trademark," she wrote in her autobiography. "I had inadvertently turned my signature into a brand."

Bloomingdale's, a department store, planned to photograph a model in a Diane von Furstenberg dress for one of its own advertisements. When the model didn't show up, someone suggested von Furstenberg pose herself. She did, and the image of her and her dress merged. "The stores would identify me and the product so closely that they would insist on featuring me in every ad," von Furstenberg wrote. "The result would be a total identity of me, the product, and the brand."

By 1976, she'd sold a million wrap dresses and landed on the cover of *Newsweek*. By 1979, her company's sales totaled $150 million

> **"THE MOST IMPORTANT RELATIONSHIP IN LIFE IS THE ONE YOU HAVE WITH YOURSELF."**

a year. "That dress paid for everything. My children's education, my houses, everything," von Furstenberg said.

But hers was not a rags-to-riches story. The Belgium-born daughter of a Holocaust survivor, von Furstenberg took her name from her first husband, an Austro-Italian prince who introduced her to Vreeland. Diane von Furstenberg could have easily lived off her husband's fortune. But early on in her first marriage, she resolved to be an independent woman, to be able to pay her own bills, and have an identity beyond being a princess.

"I did not know what I wanted to do, but I knew the kind of woman I wanted to be. I wanted to be a woman who's in charge of her life," she said. "I'm lucky I became that woman because of a little dress."

Today the brand known as DVF includes handbags, shoes, jewelry, and accessories and is sold in more than 70 countries. But von Furstenberg's design success didn't transfer into management, she said in a 2015 *New York Times* interview. Her company had just hired its first chief executive officer, and von Furstenberg admitted to never having learned to manage employees. "I am not a good CEO, but I have the passion and the force of a founder, and therefore I can make things happen," she said. "I'm a person who invented something and who invented herself."

Bridget Hilton

INCORPORATE A CAUSE

In 2012, Bridget Hilton watched a video of a woman in her twenties hearing sound for the very first time.

Hilton couldn't imagine never hearing. She'd fallen in love with music as a child and had been working in the music business for a decade, since she was a teenager. Music was her passion, her life.

"The woman in the video was my age, and it really got me thinking about how important sound and music is in my life," Hilton said. "That was the light-bulb moment of deciding I wanted to help people hear, who have never heard before."

More than 360 million people around the world suffer from disabling hearing loss, but only a tiny fraction of them can afford hearing aids. Hilton wanted to give as many people as possible the gift of sound. After brainstorming ways to build a company that could, she launched LSTN Sound Co.

LSTN was conceived as the Warby Parker of headphones. Warby Parker is a company that sells prescription glasses and sunglasses. For every pair of eyeglasses Warby Parker sells, it sees that a pair is provided to a person who needs glasses but can't afford them. LSTN makes headphones and speakers and partners with Starkey, a charity that provides hearing aids to people around the world.

Esquire magazine called LSTN headphones "quite possibly the coolest headphones . . . ever." LSTN also makes noise-canceling headsets for Delta Airlines' business-class customers. Most importantly to Hilton, since LSTN's start in 2013, the company has helped 30,000 people—many of them children—hear for the first time or for the first time in a long while.

Before she could help people with hearing impairment, Hilton needed to build a profitable company. She looked into headphones and found plenty of high-quality ones already on the market. Hers needed to be different. Most headphone ear cups are made of plastic. Hilton had another idea.

"I looked around at my piano, guitar, and all of my instruments, and they were all made of wood," she said. "I couldn't think of a better material for headphones." With wooden ear cups, Hilton's headphones would stand out on store shelves and in music lovers' minds. But she couldn't use just any wood. It had to be recycled, and it had to be beautiful. "Look good, sound good, do good," became the company's mantra.

For the charitable piece, Hilton turned to the nonprofit group Starkey. Once Starkey agreed to work with Hilton and her partner, Joe Huff, LSTN began manufacturing headphones. At that point, Hilton quit her marketing job at Universal Music Group, where she worked with some of the biggest names in music, including Eminem and Taylor Swift.

BUSINESSES THAT GIVE BACK

Many entrepreneurs focus on earning a profit. But some are known as social entrepreneurs. They create businesses to make a difference in the world. Their business models include plans to help others, improve society, or protect the environment. Bridget Hilton is one of many incredible social entrepreneurs who built a for-profit company with a mission to help people in need. Caitlin Crosby is another. She founded the Giving Keys, which provides full-time jobs for people transitioning out of homelessness. They make necklaces from engraved keys. Social entrepreneur Jenny Amaraneni launched a line of eco-friendly sunglasses called Solo Eyewear. For each pair sold, the company pays for eye care for someone in need.

"EVERY PURCHASE YOU MAKE IS **A CHANCE** TO VOTE WITH YOUR WALLET."

From the beginning, LSTN incorporated its mission into its brand. Hilton calls it a "social brand."

"My life is completely different because of the giving element of the company. Not only have we been able to help so many people hear for the first time, our lives have been so enriched," she said.

She'll never forget the faces of people she's fitted with hearing aids who experience sound for the first time. She used all her savings to fly to Peru, where she put hearing aids in the ears of Maria, who was celebrating her 18th birthday. "We fit her with hearing aids, and in 10 seconds, her world opened up," Hilton said. For the first time, Maria could hear her mother say "I love you." In Kenya, she fitted a 14-year-old girl with hearing aids. Until then, the girl's parents had kept her inside. Being able to hear freed her to go outside.

Hilton spends about one-fourth of her time on her charitable mission and the remainder on the headphone and speaker business. But she sees the mission and the business as inseparable, and the majority of her customers say that LSTN's aid to people with hearing impairment was a top reason for buying the company's products.

"Young people want to buy high-quality products with a good cause," Hilton said. "The way things are going with the trend of giving, if you don't give, you're going to look really, really bad. When you're starting a business, incorporate a cause."

Muriel "Mickie" Siebert

ROCK THE BOAT

"I put my head down and charge," is how Muriel "Mickie" Siebert once explained her legendary success as a New York City stockbroker.

After dropping out of college to care for her dying father, Siebert drove to Manhattan from her native Cleveland in 1954. She had $500 to her name. At the time, it was still rare—and not well accepted—for a woman to aspire to a career outside of teaching or nursing. Siebert, however, was drawn to finance and banking. She had first visited the New York Stock Exchange the previous year, where she remembered watching "a sea of men in dark suits" engaged in "the clamorous human buzz of . . . thousands of deals."

"Now *this* is exciting," she told her friends then. "Maybe I'll come back here and look for a job."

Siebert was turned down for one position because she didn't have a college degree. In her next interview, she lied and said she did. She was hired as a research trainee by a firm that bought and sold stocks. "I was really a glorified gofer, but you create opportunities by performing, not complaining," she later wrote.

Siebert worked her way up by paying attention and working as hard as or harder than her male colleagues. She learned as much as she could about the industries she followed. She changed jobs three times after finding out that the men in her office were being paid more than she was for the same work.

Siebert wasn't the first female stockbroker. That honor is shared by two sisters, Victoria Woodhull and Tennessee Claflin, who opened their own brokerage firm in the late nineteenth century. But in 1967, the same year Siebert opened her own brokerage firm, Muriel Siebert & Co., she became the first woman to buy a seat on the New York Stock Exchange. This prestigious and powerful position allowed her to trade stocks on its floor.

For the next ten years, Siebert was the sole woman among 1,365 men holding seats on the exchange. She went on to be the first woman to be appointed as superintendent of banking for New York.

Throughout her career, in ways large and small, Siebert boldly battled the male prejudice that would have kept her and other women on the sidelines of power and profit. In 1987, she was so furious that there was no ladies' room outside the luncheon club of the New York Stock Exchange that she threatened to have a portable toilet delivered. The new bathroom was promptly installed.

> **"I SLEEP WELL AT NIGHT, KNOWING THAT I'VE BEEN COMPETITIVE BUT HONEST, TENACIOUS BUT SCRUPULOUS, TOUGH BUT FAIR."**

Siebert never married or had children, but doted on her long-haired Chihuahua, named Monster Girl. After Monster Girl, she had Monster Girl 2. Her pets, she said proudly, weren't intimidated by the "big dogs."

Her hard work and courage helped inspire other women to follow her path. But she didn't just lead by example. She helped found the Committee of 200, a group of businesswomen who get together to network, inspire, and encourage one another. Siebert has also donated millions of dollars to help other women get their start in the finance world. For many years, she campaigned for more financial literacy for women, investing more than $1 million to develop a personal finance course for high school students.

When it came to her own achievements, Siebert never failed to credit the value of hard work. "I didn't create my business simply by pounding on the door and saying 'I'm a woman, I'm entitled,'" she has said. "I made my success by slugging it out with the boys."

STOCK MARKET 101

If you buy stock in a company, it means you own a portion of that company. Stock prices go up or down depending on how well a company is doing. People can make money by buying stocks if they hold onto them until the stocks rise in value and then sell them. But it isn't that easy. If a company's profits fall, the stock price will fall.

The stock market is where you buy and sell stocks. And there isn't just one market. The largest U.S. markets are the New York Stock Exchange and the Nasdaq, in New York City. A stockbroker, like Muriel Siebert, is a person authorized to buy and sell stocks through the stock market. In order to make money for their clients, stockbrokers research companies, study the news, and try to make smart decisions about when to buy and sell.

For many years, people would spend a lot of money to hire a stockbroker in order to gain access to the stock market. But now that stocks are available for purchase online, many people do that for themselves.

31

Katrina Lake

FIND AN UNMET NEED AND **FILL IT**

When you see celebrities and models in magazines or catalogs, you can be sure they didn't pick out their own outfits. Someone called a stylist chose every item of their clothing, and maybe even helped to dress them. Stylists dress pretty much every person you see in print or on a red carpet, tucking in a shirt just so, rolling up sleeves, buttoning the right number of buttons, or pairing a dress with the perfect necklace.

Now, thanks to Katrina Lake, you don't have to be rich or famous anymore to have your own stylist. Lake's company, Stitch Fix, collects information from its customers and then matches them with stylists who choose clothing and accessories just for them.

In November 2017, at the age of 34, Lake became the youngest woman founder of a business to "go public." When a company goes public, the owners ask investors to buy shares in their company to help it grow. As Lake stood on stage at the ceremony on Wall Street, she held her 14-month-old son on her hip. She was blazing a trail not only as a woman but also as a mother.

As an undergraduate at Stanford University, Lake studied biology. She thought she might be a doctor, like her father. But she soon realized, "I didn't really love being around gross stuff, and I couldn't imagine wearing a lab coat and *scrubs* every day." Fun, good-looking

> **"I WANTED TO WORK AT THE RETAILER OF THE FUTURE. WHEN I DIDN'T SEE IT, I REALIZED THAT I COULD START IT MYSELF."**

clothes were a lot more interesting to her.

In college, she would often call her older sister (who later became a buyer for high-end fashion brands like Elie Tahari and Pucci) for fashion advice. Pretty soon, Lake started wondering why other women couldn't find such a helpful, time-saving service online.

Lake went on to business school at Harvard University, where she continued to look around for the company she imagined. She couldn't find anything like it. So, in 2011, she created it herself.

Stitch Fix serves the same purpose as Lake's calls to her sister. First, you fill out a detailed online quiz about your style, fit, and the amount you want to spend. Then, for a $20 fee, your personal stylist picks out five pieces of clothing, shoes, and accessories for you to try on at home. Each package comes with a prepaid envelope so you can send back whatever you don't like. Stitch Fix also earns a percentage of the cost of all of the clothing that shoppers decide to keep. You can choose to receive a single box, or you can receive automatic deliveries from once every two to three weeks to once every three months.

Stitch Fix stylists get help from computer algorithms that compare the customer's profile to an inventory of items from more than 1,000 brands. The computer program helps them pinpoint a list of items the customer will be most likely to love.

Within just six years of its launch date, Stitch Fix had become a "unicorn." That is what the tech industry calls a start-up company valued at more than $1 billion. Stitch Fix is now worth more than twice that amount, with 5,800 employees (including thousands of stylists) and several distribution centers, serving both male and female shoppers.

Lake has said that her tremendous success has been "a struggle every step of the way." At first, neither her Harvard professors nor the investors she initially courted understood what she was trying to do. Many of them were men, and they couldn't seem to understand the appeal of having a personal shopper. Lake simply persevered until she proved them wrong. She understood the time pressure on women who want to look put together, even if the men she spoke to didn't.

Once she raised the money, Lake still faced some tough problems. She had a falling out with a business partner, who sued her (they later settled for an undisclosed sum). She also acknowledged that, early on, she had trouble maintaining inventory. She didn't always have the right number of items in the right sizes available when customers wanted them. But the more data Stitch Fix collected from customers, the more the company knew about what styles, colors, and sizes people wanted, which helped to solve the inventory problem.

Creating and running Stitch Fix has given Lake increasing confidence that she can figure out things on her own. Lake believes that getting dressed can help people "set the stage" for success. "When you feel great, when you feel your best, it opens up a world of possibility," she said. "Feeling confident and self-assured are important inputs into good days, successful days, and happy days."

Judy Faulkner

NERDS RULE

Growing up in New Jersey in the 1950s, Judy Faulkner loved science and math. Math, in particular, fascinated her, with its unshakable truths about patterns and relationships.

There weren't many girls who shared her interests, and Faulkner got teased for being a nerd. It was all so painful that some thirty years later, she was thrilled to watch Bill Gates rise to fame as the cofounder of Microsoft. "He made being nerdy a good thing," she has said.

By then, Faulkner was already well on her way to making her own fortune, as a founder and CEO of Epic Systems, America's largest health-record software company. Headquartered in Wisconsin, Epic supplies medical records for more than half of all Americans and has offices in several foreign countries. Its prestigious U.S. clients include the Mayo Clinic and the Johns Hopkins Medical Center. One of its popular products, MyChart, lets patients track their health records and communicate with doctors.

Faulkner established the company in 1979 in a Madison basement, in collaboration with two of her former professors at the University of Wisconsin–Madison. After taking one of the nation's first classes combining computer science and medicine, she was inspired to do research that led to the creation of Epic's early software, a program called Patient Information, Storage and Retrieval.

Eleven years after it was founded, Epic had only 30 employees. But even then, it was starting to acquire impressive clients such as the Harvard Community Health Plan and the Ontario Ministry of Health in Canada. Growth really took off after it rolled out EpicCare, a highly successful web-based app that lets doctors and patients safely share access to medical and billing records.

By 2018, Epic had more than 9,000 employees and annual revenues of $2.7 billion. At 73, Faulkner was reported to be worth more than $3.5 billion, making her the wealthiest self-made American woman in the tech industry. "The work of my life has been to develop software that would help keep people well and help sick people get better," she has said. "I never had any personal desire to be a wealthy billionaire."

A major factor in Faulkner's extraordinary success has been the same willingness to be different that marked her teenage years. She trusts her instincts, even when they lead her down paths few others follow. For instance, while many entrepreneurs welcome outside investment in their firms to help them grow, Faulkner has rejected this path. She has said she's not willing to give up any control over her company to investors who may be more interested in profits than doing what's best for the company and its employees.

Faulkner's wardrobe choices are also unconventional. She won't wear high heels, and she contends that stockings "constrain your

WOMEN IN STEM

Women in the United States have 47 percent of the available jobs, but only 24 percent of the STEM jobs. The good news is that women who go into STEM fields on average earn more money than both men and women in similar jobs in other fields. What kinds of jobs count as STEM jobs? Here are just a few: computer scientist, astronomer, food scientist, nuclear engineer, environmental engineer, naval architect, chemical technician, and geologist.

> **"WHY DO YOU COME TO WORK?
> FOR THE PAYCHECK?
> FOR SOMETHING INTERESTING TO DO?
> FOR CUSTOMERS?
> FOR THE COMPETITION?
> FOR THE MISSION?
> IF I HAD TO CIRCLE ONE REASON,
> IT'S FOR MY CUSTOMERS."**

thinking." But she shows up each year at the company's annual client meeting in fun costumes that have included Supergirl, a Harley-Davidson biker, and the Mad Hatter from *Alice in Wonderland*. Faulkner set up shop, early on, in an old Victorian building instead of a conventional glass office tower. She wanted to create an environment where working all night in your pajamas felt natural.

Faulkner may still be nerdy, but nerdiness is now her brand—and a winning one. One of her biggest regrets is that her two daughters (now adults) have shied away from the STEM fields of science, technology, engineering, and math, even though, as she says, they were good at them. "They absolutely refused to take any classes in computer science, or to learn to program," she has said. "And the reason is, they said it was too nerdy, and they didn't want to be nerdy. And I felt really bad about that. I thought, 'Wow, it's such a good field.' It's a shame they didn't at least explore it. Because it would have been fun."

Ursula Burns

EMBRACE STEM

Ursula Burns recalls her mother telling her and her siblings that "*where* we were was not *who* we were." She listened, refusing to let her childhood in a New York City housing project curb her ambition. Her mother took in laundry to help send her kids to private Catholic schools. But when Burns' teachers tried to steer her to one of three careers—nurse, teacher, or nun—Burns chose a fourth option. High school tests showed that she was good at math, so she studied to be a mechanical engineer. Three decades later, Burns was running one of the world's largest businesses, as CEO of Xerox. She was the first black woman to head a Fortune 500 company. Her degree, she has said, was the key to her success.

Burns first worked for Xerox as a summer intern, in 1980. Later, she said, she "accidentally" moved into the business side after realizing she needed to know more about her customers. "I had to learn how this great set of solutions that I was developing would be priced, who would buy it, and how it would be used," she has said. "As a result, I became more and more familiar with business elements. . . . As I did that, I got paid more money, and the world of business became more and more interesting."

While Burns was moving up in her career, the corporate world was coming under pressure to become more inclusive and hire more women and people of color. Some companies—like Xerox—were more responsive than others. "Thirty years ago, when I started working—literally, the chances of me making it were worse than minuscule," Burns has said. "We should be saying 'hooray' to the people of Xerox. We should be giving them a medal."

In her early years of working at Xerox, Burns says she was one of "very, very few women" and even fewer black women at the company. But no one seemed to mind what she described as the "huge Afro" she sported then. Instead, she said, her managers just focused on how she was doing her job. "What they said was, 'I'm going to give you an opportunity, and if you can work hard enough and learn fast enough and really be driven and focused, you are going to go a long way,'" she has said.

Burns stayed on as CEO of Xerox through 2016, when the company split into two separate divisions. When she left Xerox, there still wasn't a single other African-American woman at the helm of any of the leading 500 U.S. companies. U.S. corporations still have a long way to go to become more diverse, she acknowledges. But for now, she believes women should take advantage of opportunities to stand out as "one of the few."

In 2009, President Barack Obama appointed Burns to help lead the White House National STEM education initiative, a position she held for several years. She encouraged other women to study STEM fields, to seek STEM-focused jobs, and to organize themselves to wield more power. "I guarantee you that you will be the minority in the room," she has said. "And instead of that being a burden, it should be an opportunity for you to distinguish yourself."

> **"PEOPLE ARE MORE LIKELY TO BE SUCCESSFUL IF THEY HAVE A PASSION FOR WHAT THEY DO."**

Tavi Gevinson

FIND YOUR VOICE

When Tavi Gevinson was 13, she dyed her hair ice blue. For some girls, it might have been a passing fad. For Gevinson, it was one more declaration of the independent style at the center of her extraordinary career.

Gevinson rose to fame after creating *Style Rookie*, a fashion blog, at age 11. It featured lots of pictures of her that showed off her unique fashion sense. Over the years, Gevinson has been photographed wearing an absurdly giant purple bow as a hat, a shiny green paisley miniskirt, and bright-red plaid stockings. "In my opinion, the most interesting fashion is the Anti-Fashion," she wrote when she was 12. "No rules, no restrictions, no normalcy, no *pleasing anyone* . . ."

The combination of Gevinson's eccentric wardrobe and quirky thoughts about clothes and her life as a suburban, middle-class middle schooler was a hit. Lady Gaga called her "the future of journalism." She was spotted in the front row of Dior's Spring 2010 Couture fashion show in Paris. *POP* magazine flew her to Tokyo, Japan, to interview designer Rei Kawakubo. She and her mother were guests of honor at a party for the fashion label Comme des Garçons. *Teen Vogue* called her "the luckiest 13-year-old on the planet."

But since then, Gevinson has been busy proving that luck had little to do with it, and has pushed herself to meet new and bigger

challenges. At the age of 15, she launched *Rookie*, an online magazine for teens. (Within a week, it got a million page views.) At 16, she was in a movie with Julia Louis-Dreyfus. At 18, she was starring in a Broadway show alongside Michael Cera.

Writing and editing are Gevinson's ways of making cultural change. She uses them to keep challenging a society that tends to talk down to teens. Of mainstream teen magazines, she has said: "I feel like if I followed their articles about boys and truly believed it was as important to do certain things or avoid certain things as they say, I would probably go crazy. Sometimes their 'embarrassing' stories are literally about boys finding out that you have your period."

Rookie featured articles that Gevinson saw as much more in tune with her readers' inner lives, with titles like, "On Taking Yourself Seriously," "How to Not Care What People Think of You," "How to Manage Your Social Media Intake," and "How to Look Like You Weren't Just Crying in Less than Five Minutes."

Gevinson has built her successful career with a keen sense of style, exceptional writing talent, and a lot of hard work. And she recognizes that continuing to stay fresh and original is a challenge. "I think a lot of people freeze at the age that they become successful, whether they're younger or older, just because it's like the universe is saying, 'You've done everything right up until this point, and you don't have to change a thing, and you don't have to evolve,'" she has said. "And that's usually where the flame goes out. I've tried to avoid that."

> **"I'M NOT A FEARLESS PERSON BY ANY MEANS, BUT I ALWAYS FIND THAT THE FEAR OF HOLDING MYSELF BACK ALWAYS OUTWEIGHS THE FEAR OF WHAT COULD HAPPEN BY DOING SOMETHING."**

Mariam Naficy

LET THE CUSTOMER CHOOSE AND STAY FRESH FOREVER

Mariam Naficy loves to shop. "I've been a lifelong shopper," she said. "As a girl, I would do a lot of homework. Then I would always go to the mall and window shop. And I would think, first this brand is hot, then it's not."

One after another, the clothing designers she idolized as a teenager fell out of fashion. On a quest to find a way to build a brand that would stay fresh forever, Naficy had an idea. She would crowdsource the design of a line of products.

Enter Minted, an online stationery company she built in 2007. Artists submit their work to the site, designers and customers vote on their favorite pieces, and Minted sells the winners.

The company started selling wedding invitations and branched out into holiday cards. Now Minted is a complete art, stationery, and home décor marketplace. It offers framed art, photographs, and styling services. One of their stylists might help you pick a piece of art to hang over your bed or choose a frame for your favorite puppy photo.

Minted was Naficy's second start-up. She sold her first, an online cosmetics company called Eve.com, for more than $100 million in 2000. She was 29. After she paid off the investors and her partner took her share, the sale made Naficy a multimillionaire. But she wanted a new challenge. She also wanted to prove to herself that she wasn't just lucky with Eve.com. "Once you're lucky; twice you're good," she said. "You have to do it a second time."

Naficy had studied successful brands, like the Gap. She learned that hiring the right people to choose the merchandise was key to staying in style. But even top product pickers have bad seasons. As long as individuals selected the merchandise, the business would be subject to ever-changing customer whims. But what if every customer could have a say, Naficy wondered. "The hypothesis was that if you turn all of the decisions over to the crowd, you will be potentially fresh forever," she said.

At Minted, Naficy confirmed her hypothesis. Crowdsourcing works. As of 2018, the San Francisco–based company was bringing in hundreds of millions of dollars in revenue a year.

She credits Minted's success to consumers being able to choose the products. "They're voting with their pocketbooks," she said.

Most of the artists who enter Minted's design competitions have other sources of income. One Minted artist is a mortician, another woman is a plumber. "We're like a big talent agency," Naficy said. A few of the artists earn enough from the work they sell to Minted to support themselves. But most use the money they earn on the site to supplement their income or maybe pay for a vacation.

Naficy started Minted with money she raised from friends or angel investors. By 2018, she had raised $90 million in capital.

ANGEL INVESTORS

The term *angel investor* originally was used to describe investors in Broadway shows. They provided money to keep shows running, knowing that they might never get their money back. Now, angels invest in all industries, from health care to software. Angels invest their own money in start-up companies in exchange for the chance to own a piece of a business that may someday be valuable. Most angels are not millionaires. They are often friends or colleagues who want to help an entrepreneur succeed.

When she graduated from Williams College, Naficy thought "real entrepreneurs don't go to business school." But she changed her mind. She decided that a solid grounding in business would be useful. She went on to earn a master's in business administration at Stanford University.

The connections she made at Stanford have been extremely useful for Naficy, particularly for raising money to launch her start-ups. "The network really helped me," she said. "I think it helps women a lot with tapping into fundraising because it's a little bit harder to be taken seriously."

> "A MOTIVATED WOMAN WITH A NETWORK IS A POWERFUL COMBINATION."

At first, Naficy had trouble convincing investors that crowdsourcing would work. "We almost went under so many times. We almost ran out of cash over and over again," she said. Yet she hung on. "Part of it was believing in the idea of crowdsourcing," she said. "I loved the mission and really did believe in it."

She was right. Her proof is in the profit.

BE **WILLING** TO CHANGE

As any entrepreneur knows, it's a huge help when lots of people know your name.

Consider Oprah Winfrey. She built her multibillion-dollar business empire by connecting with millions of devoted fans who recognize her simply as "Oprah." She hosted *The Oprah Winfrey Show* for 25 years, and it became the highest-rated national talk show of all time. Her glossy national magazine, *O*, features her face on its cover. And she became the first African-American woman to own a cable network when she launched OWN: Oprah Winfrey Network in January 2011.

Oprah's success is all the more stunning when you know what led up to it. She was born into such poverty, in rural Mississippi, that she attended school wearing dresses sewn from potato sacks. Growing up, however, she learned discipline, optimism, and uncommon resilience. "You may not be responsible for being down, but you have to be responsible for getting up," she said. "That is why I am where I am. Because bad things have happened in my life and I'd just get up and say, 'Do the best you can.'"

Oprah often celebrated these virtues on her TV show, which started in 1986 and ran for more than 4,500 episodes. The program featured a mixture of celebrity interviews and self-help and spiritual advice. Oprah became an influential voice on issues, including child abuse, drug addiction, and civil rights. All the while, she maintained a bond with her audience by openly discussing her personal battles to lose weight and recover from childhood abuse.

In May 2011, when the final episode of her talk show aired, Oprah had no intention of retiring. She moved to California to take a more hands-on role with her network, whose early ratings had fallen short of what she had expected.

As Oprah later acknowledged, the problem was that she'd wrongly assumed her audience would be open to a full-time schedule of self-help shows, including yoga and meditation lessons. But many viewers weren't interested. "I had a vision of what living your best life could look like," Oprah said. "The people told me otherwise. I had to redo my vision." She launched a new show featuring one-on-one conversations between herself and inspiring business leaders, pop culture icons, and other influential people. Among other things, that gave viewers more of what they had missed—namely her.

Within two years, the network was making a profit. By 2017, when Oprah sold a portion of her stake in the business, OWN was hailed as a major success.

Oprah also decided to use her time to return to the big screen, acting in and producing films such as *Selma*, *The Immortal Life of Henrietta Lacks*, and *A Wrinkle in Time*.

Oprah has acknowledged that her journey has been humbling. Yet she always makes a point of learning from adversity. The main lesson, she has said, is to remain willing to change.

"Challenges are gifts that force us to search for a new center of gravity," she says. "Don't fight them. Just find a new way to stand."

> "**THE BEST SECRET IN LIFE IS THAT THERE'S NO BIG SECRET. WHATEVER YOUR AIMS, YOU WILL GET THERE IF YOU'RE WILLING TO WORK.**"

Reese Witherspoon

LEVERAGE SUCCESS

Reese Witherspoon began her acting career at age 14. She is probably best known for her starring roles in front of the camera. But after more than 25 years working in Hollywood, she discovered a powerful role *behind* the scenes, producing movies that showcase strong women as screenwriters, directors, and actors.

Witherspoon began producing movies in 2000, with credits including *Legally Blonde 2*, *Penelope*, and *Hot Pursuit*. In 2016, she founded a new production company, Hello Sunshine, dedicated to "discovering content that celebrates women and puts them at the center of the story."

She said she'd gotten tired of hearing other producers tell her that audiences had a limited appetite for movies about strong women characters. What's more, she didn't believe them. "Women want to see themselves on screen, and they don't want to see this very one-dimensional wife or girlfriend of a superhero," she has said. "They want to see mothers and teenagers and different aspects of femininity on film."

Like the heroines of her favorite stories, Witherspoon decided she wasn't going to wait for events or other people to change things. She began a telephone lobbying campaign to recruit support for women writers, producers, and stars of all ages and colors.

"Instead of having people make calls for me, I called every studio head myself," she has said. "'Hey, it's Reese!' I've known everybody for 27 years. . . . I've made movies at pretty much every studio."

By leveraging her stardom in that way, Witherspoon boosted Hello Sunshine's fortunes. The company negotiated three deals with Apple, as Apple set out to compete with Netflix and Amazon in making new shows and movies for its streaming service. Apple pledged roughly $240 million—an enormous sum—for a single series starring Witherspoon and Jennifer Aniston as cohosts of a fictional news program. The two other projects were a comedy series starring Kristen Wiig and a drama series starring Octavia Spencer. Hello Sunshine also produced a movie about the first African-American woman to graduate from Vassar College.

> "YOU CAN SIT THERE AND COMPLAIN ABOUT IT, OR YOU CAN **DO SOMETHING ABOUT IT.**"

"I've done enough for myself," Witherspoon has said. "I had a whole great career." Now she's determined to give other women a boost and improve her industry's culture. "I'm using everything I've learned along the way and my own money and celebrity collateral—whatever that is—and I will stand next to anyone I believe in that deserves a different opportunity," she has said. "And that's thrilling to me! I wake up every day, and I turn to my assistant and go, 'I love this company.'"

STRONG FEMALE LEADS

Reese Witherspoon is right! People want to see movies about women. In 2017, the movie industry was surprised by the blockbuster success of the movie *Wonder Woman*. Only two other movies made more money in the United States and Canada that year: the live-action *Beauty and the Beast* and *Star Wars: The Last Jedi*. All three of these films feature strong, smart women in starring roles.

Josephine Cochrane

TIMING IS EVERYTHING

Have you heard the expression "necessity is the mother of invention"? It applies perfectly to Josephine Cochrane and her 1885 brainchild—the automatic dishwasher. And it means that if you really need something, you'll figure out a way to get it or make it yourself.

A wealthy socialite, Cochrane began throwing dinner parties in her mansion-like home in Shelbyville, Illinois, in the 1870s. Servants set the dining room table with her family's 200-year-old china. When the guests finished eating, the help cleared the heirloom dishes and scrubbed them by hand. After one party, Cochrane noticed that some of her plates were chipped. She scolded her employees and insisted they never touch her fine china again.

She wasn't about to ask her husband to wash the dishes. It was the 1880s, after all, and housework was considered women's work. So she took over the job herself, soaping and rinsing each plate, cup, and saucer. The task soon grew tiresome, not to mention her chapped hands. One day, Cochrane examined a cup and thought that there must be a better way.

She set to work designing an automatic dishwasher. Some say she might have inherited a talent for mechanics from her father, a civil engineer, and her great-grandfather, a steamboat builder. Soon after she began drafting her plans, in 1883, her husband died. To her surprise, he left her nearly penniless. Now, at 44 years old, she needed to build a machine not just to wash her own dishes but also to provide her with an income.

Cochrane's concept was simple—aim water jets at dishes held firmly in wire racks. She put the racks into a cylindrical cage and lowered it into a copper boiler, which heated the water. A hand-powered lever pumped jets of soapy water and then clean water onto the dishes.

With eight pages of drawings, Cochrane applied for a patent on New Year's Eve in 1885, and she was awarded one a year later. To this day, her design remains the blueprint for one of the greatest laborsaving inventions ever. But inventing a product, she learned, was easy compared to selling it.

"When it comes to buying something for the kitchen that costs $75 or $100, a woman begins at once to figure out all the other things she could do with the money," she said. Plus, men, who often controlled the family's money, were unwilling to buy a costly kitchen appliance for a chore their wives did

SECURING A PATENT

If you have an invention that is unique and useful, you can apply for a patent like Josephine Cochrane did. You'll need to file paperwork with the U.S. Patent and Trademark Office (USPTO). In addition to coming up with a name and description for your invention, you will need to explain the problem it solves or the process it improves. If you're able to make your case and earn a patent, it means that nobody can copy your idea. So if you have the first and only machine that automatically makes your bed every morning, you might be able to make a lot of money off of your brilliant invention! (But be warned: it can take two years or longer to get a patent approved.)

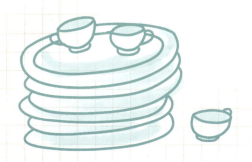

for free. Americans did not want to shell out the money to buy dishwashers for their home kitchens until the 1950s, long after Cochrane died.

The timing was not right for selling to families. So Cochrane aimed for the commercial market—hotels and restaurants. But first she had to muster the courage to enter the businesses.

"You cannot imagine what it was like in those days . . . for a woman to cross a hotel lobby alone. I had never been anywhere without my husband or father," she said. "The lobby seemed a mile wide. I thought I should faint at every step, but I didn't—and I got an $800 order as my reward."

The timing was just right for restaurants and hotels to buy Cochrane's machine. And, in 1893, her dishwasher got a major promotional boost when it won first place for best mechanical construction at the Chicago World's Fair.

Although she never cracked the home market, Cochrane's time-saving invention lives on. Some even credit the dishwasher with helping women break out of the kitchen and into the workplace. After her death in 1913 at the age of 74, the Hobart Manufacturing Company purchased her company. In 1949, the company introduced home dishwashers under the KitchenAid brand—the same brand that might clean your dishes tonight.

> **"WOMEN ARE INVENTIVE, THE COMMON OPINION TO THE CONTRARY NOTWITHSTANDING."**

KICK-START YOUR DREAM

Debbie Sterling makes the toys she wished she had when she was a girl.

She would have enjoyed playing with Lego, K'NEX, or Lincoln Logs. But she considered them "boys' toys." A friend she met while studying engineering at Stanford University said that playing with construction toys as a child helped develop her interest in the field. When Sterling was a kid, companies marketed construction toys to boys. Could that be why more boys were interested in STEM subjects, Sterling wondered. "I started to think that maybe the fact that in our culture girls play with dolls and boys play with building sets is one of the reasons why so few women enter into the field of engineering," she said.

Sterling began to conceive of GoldieBlox—a combination storybook and construction set.

Goldie and her crew go on adventures and solve problems by building simple machines. The construction materials are cast in purple, yellow, and pink. As girls read along, they use their tool kits to build what Goldie builds. Goldie resembles the strong, confident yet flawed heroines Sterling met in books she read as a child. She could be a cross between Pippi Longstocking and Matilda.

Sterling tested her idea on more than 100 kids. Girls wanted

GoldieBlox. "But the toy industry wasn't as receptive," she said. "I kept hearing from industry veterans that my idea was a good cause, but it would never sell."

Unable to convince stores to stock her toys, Sterling launched a Kickstarter campaign in 2012. In a video, she introduced herself and her creation. "I'm starting a toy company called GoldieBlox to get little girls to love engineering as much as I do," she said. "To me, GoldieBlox really is the toy I wish I had growing up."

She sat cross-legged on a living room floor, held up a sample of the pastel-colored toy, and urged viewers to order one. "Buy these for your daughter, your niece, your friend's daughter. Any girl you know is so much more than just a princess," she said. Then she tiptoed down the aisle of a toy store, placed a picture of Goldie in front of a Barbie box, and pleaded: "Help me build GoldieBlox so that our girls can help build the future."

Within three months, GoldieBlox had $1 million in preorders. By 2018, more than 1 million of the toys had been sold around the world.

CROWDFUNDING

One way for an entrepreneur to raise money without taking out loans is to use a crowdfunding site like Kickstarter, Indiegogo, RocketHub, or Crowdfunder. Piggybackr is one of the crowdfunding sites that welcomes fundraisers of all ages. (Most require fundraisers to be 18 or older.)

To create a fundraising campaign, you upload text, pictures, and videos that explain your idea, how much money you need, and what you will do with it. Then you share the campaign with friends, family, and anyone you think might be interested. People who want to support your idea or business will make a donation. Some people donate to campaigns for nothing in return or for a small thank-you gift. Some campaigns offer up their products as thank-you gifts for donations of certain amounts. Debbie Sterling offered a GoldieBlox construction set, complete with book and character figurines, for donations of $30 or more. In the end, 5,519 donors contributed to her Kickstarter campaign. She raised $285,881 to make GoldieBlox!

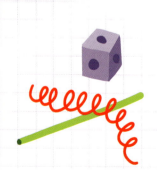

"The campaign went viral overnight," Sterling said. "It was clear that there was an appetite for GoldieBlox products and our greater social mission."

That mission, to spark girls' interest in engineering, continues to motivate Sterling. It also continues to throw up challenges.

"I knew that if I wanted to make GoldieBlox successful, it meant I had to break down the outdated gender stereotypes that plague the industry," she said. "To this day, these outdated stereotypes continue to be my biggest challenge."

For example, Sterling held a question-and-answer session offering tips for empowering women in technology during an Apple conference. She was happy to see men in the audience, but the men wound up talking over all the women. Challenges like this only reinforce Sterling's desire to let girls know they have limitless possibilities. To that end, she's started a GoldieBlox campaign to celebrate fearless women—women like the African-American mathematicians who played a vital role in the early U.S. space mission and were featured in the movie *Hidden Figures*.

"Girls can't rule the world until someone shows them how," a video launching the campaign said. "All they need is a role model to #BeLikeHer."

Sterling is an engineer, a CEO, and one awesome role model.

> **"THE MORE PEOPLE YOU TALK TO, THE MORE YOU WILL FIND THOSE WHO ARE INSPIRED BY WHAT YOU WANT TO DO AND WANT TO BE A PART OF IT. THAT IS REALLY THE KEY TO BECOMING A SUCCESSFUL ENTREPRENEUR."**

BE YOUR OWN **SUPERHERO**

Lilly Singh had plans. After she graduated from York University in Toronto, Canada, with a psychology degree, she thought she'd go on to earn a master's degree in counseling—and marry as soon as possible.

But thoughts of her future—and working toward a degree she was not passionate about—depressed her. "I lost my appetite and my desire to wake up in the morning," she said. "As scary as it sounds, I can honestly say that I lost my desire to live."

Then, in 2010, during her third year of college, she discovered YouTube. She began making and posting videos as IISuperwomanII. Her goal was to make girls and young women laugh while empowering them to be their own authentic selves—their own superheroes. Within three years, she had 1 million subscribers.

Viewers related to her videos. She talked about relationships, parents, dating, and self-empowerment. Singh felt a return of her childhood creativity and found a purpose. Her depression lifted.

"I started on YouTube because I was sad and because I wanted to make myself happy. In turn, other people also were cheered up by my videos. So it was this beautiful harmony of a community being created that was supporting me, and I was supporting them," she said.

Singh might look like an overnight success. But she doesn't see it that way. Her first video got only 70 views. "I wouldn't say it took off quickly," she told *Canadian Business*. "I'm not a product of a viral video. . . . It was pretty gradual."

Steadily and methodically, Singh built her platform. Every week, she made sure to post two new vlogs, or video blog posts, with embarrassing but hilarious life lessons. Every time she posted a vlog, she notified her followers. And the key to her popularity? "I think my channel is as successful as it is because, more than anything, it's relatable," Singh said. "I have the type of content that's shareable, where people watch it and think: 'Oh my God, we totally do this,' or 'I'm so like this,' or 'Hey, remember we were talking about this? Let me share this with my friend.'"

Singh's high-energy videos jump from scene to scene. She races around but frequently goes nowhere. Her mood changes every few seconds. But she's always herself.

In "My REAL Morning Routine," the camera zooms in on Singh in bed. Her alarm rings, and she repeatedly hits snooze. Does she have time to shower, she wonders aloud. She sniffs her armpits, tells herself "I'm fine," and decides

MAKING MONEY ON YOUTUBE

Before they can watch a video on YouTube, viewers often have to sit through an advertisement. Those ads bring in a lot of money for YouTube—and for video creators. A company asks YouTube to run their ads and pays for every thousand views. YouTube takes about 45 percent of that money. The rest goes to the creator of the video that runs after the ad.

If you want to try to make money on YouTube, you'll need to get at least 1,000 subscribers, and viewers will need to watch 4,000 hours of your videos over a 12-month period. You'll need to set yourself up as a YouTube Partner and apply for a Google account that lets you be part of Google's advertising network. Setting up the accounts is the easy part. The hard part is creating content that attracts enough viewers to make money!

You can also sell products on YouTube, ask your fans for donations, or work with brands as an influencer. Companies pay influencers to use their products, wear their clothes, or review their merchandise in videos and other social media posts.

to skip it. Rushing, she brushes her teeth, examines pimples, and pledges to drink more water. "Spoiler alert," she adds. "I won't."

Forbes named Singh the highest-paid female YouTube star in 2017, when she earned $10.5 million. By early 2018, Singh had more than 13 million subscribers, and her videos had scored billions of views.

> "YOU CONTROL YOUR DAY. YOU HAVE 24 HOURS. WHAT WILL YOU DO WITH IT?"

She'd like her success to inspire her viewers, but she wants them to know it hasn't come easily. She writes and directs her own sketches. She had to learn how to use lighting, cameras, sound, and graphics to make the most compelling vlogs. She spent years reading every one of her subscribers' comments and analyzing data about her videos to figure out why some went viral and others went nowhere. She maximized her exposure to new fans by strategically partnering with other YouTube stars. And after her career took off, she continued to grow her audience by partnering with Hollywood celebrities—from Will Smith and John Legend to Charlize Theron and Chelsea Handler.

Instead of becoming a counselor, Singh has become a role model. "We're in this unique time with social media and cute quotes on Instagram. . . . Everyone just feels so validated all of the time," she said. "There's this idea that people have to wish and hope for their dreams, but I want to bring back the art of working for them."

Mikaila Ulmer

YOU'RE NEVER **TOO YOUNG** TO START A BUSINESS

Mikaila Ulmer launched her amazing career when she was just 4 years old.

Dressed up in a bumblebee suit and with a big yellow daisy in her hair, Mikaila sold lemonade at a children's business fair in her hometown of Austin, Texas. She made the drink by adding honey to her great-grandmother's recipe, which contains flaxseeds. Together, the lemonade—and Mikaila—were such a hit that Mikaila decided she wanted to sell her lemonade at stores year-round and not just a few times a year. Her mother, a marketing expert, later encouraged her to start her own company.

Today, Mikaila's Me & the Bees Lemonade comes with extra benefits for the environment. The 13-year-old's company uses local ingredients and helps spread the word about threats to the bees that help make her honey.

Mikaila didn't always appreciate bees. Like many kids her age, she's been stung more than once. But in the course of building her business, she became interested in bees. She learned about how bees help the environment, and soon she had the makings of a mission. Bees are pollinators. By moving pollen from one plant to another, they help the plants produce new seeds, creating fruit and new plants. Pollinators help about one-third of American crops, contributing several billion dollars a year to U.S. agriculture. Yet in recent years, as Mikaila learned, honeybees have faced challenges, including disease, mites, and the increased use of pesticides. Scientists worry that they may die out entirely.

Mikaila's company's website, which features a picture of her in a beekeeper outfit, notes that Me & the Bees Lemonade contributes to several organizations working to help preserve the bees' future. "Buy a bottle . . . save a bee!" is its motto. She has also started her own nonprofit, Heathy Hive Foundation, committed to education, protection, and preservation of the bee population.

As Mikaila has moved from grade school to middle school, she has continued to be her company's ambassador. She has visited the White House twice—first to have lunch with President Barack Obama and First Lady Michelle Obama and later to join the White House Easter Egg Roll, where she served President Obama a glass of her lemonade. "I'll be back on the job market in seven months," Obama joked after meeting her, "So I hope she is hiring!"

In 2015, at the age of 9, Mikaila went on the show *Shark Tank*. Standing next to a lemonade stand, she wore a bright-yellow sundress, a teal headband, and a confident smile. "I got a sweet deal for you," she told the panel. "I created a product that is both good for you and tastes great at the same time."

One of the judges, Daymond John, was so taken by Mikaila's performance that he jumped out of his chair to give her a hug. "She was and is the face of the brand—the sweetest

WHAT IS SHARK TANK?

In this popular reality show, contestants present their ideas to a group of experienced businesspeople (known as "Sharks"). They try to convince the Sharks to invest in their business. Usually the investments come in the form of money and mentorship. Any investment comes with a price, though. If the investor and the contestant do a deal, then the investor will usually end up owning a portion of the contestant's company.

"EVEN AS KIDS, WE'RE CAPABLE OF DOING SO MUCH."

little thing in the world!" he later said. John invested $60,000 in the new company, in return for a 25 percent share. That was Mikaila's big break. Sales took off, and distribution increased from 35 stores in Austin to more than 200 stores throughout the United States. Mikaila's picture is on every label.

Like many other young entrepreneurs, Mikaila has gotten lots of help from her talented family. Her mother, D'Andra, founded her own marketing firm before becoming "Chief Marketing Bee" for Me & the Bees Lemonade in 2014. Her dad, Theo, a financial consultant, also helps out.

Mikaila spends lots of her time on her business, juggling travel, speaking engagements, and interviews with school, homework, and fun. She enjoys birthday parties and sleepovers as much as any other kid. Yet after nearly a decade at work, she doesn't seem to be slowing down. "I'm going to take it step by step and day by day and see what comes out of it," she said in a recent interview.

Mikaila's advice for other young entrepreneurs is simple: "Dream big," she says. "Dream like a kid."

REWARD YOUR CUSTOMERS

How did Estée Lauder become a trailblazer, marketing genius, cosmetics billionaire, and household name?

Partly by giving away a lot of free stuff.

Estée Lauder was born Josephine Esther Mentzer. Growing up, she lived with her Eastern European Jewish immigrant parents above her father's hardware store in Queens, in New York City. When she was still a teenager in the 1920s, she took an interest in the face creams that her chemist uncle, John Schotz, concocted over his gas stove. She got her start in business by helping him market them. She named one of his early blends Super Rich All-Purpose Cream and began by selling it to her friends.

The young future mogul had watched her father give away hammers and nails to his customers for Christmas. So she understood the appeal of free samples. She began visiting nearby beauty salons to give out little gifts of cold cream to women as they waited under hair dryers, winning over her first loyal customers.

Lauder's marketing talent was ahead of her time. Marketing experts say that giving free samples remains one of the most effective ways to introduce new products to customers.

From those early days, Lauder truly believed in her products. She was convinced that once other women tried them out, they'd want to buy them. "I love to touch the creams, smell them, look at them, carry them with me," she has said. "A person has to love her harvest if she's to expect others to love it."

In 1930, Mentzer married Joseph Lauter, who later changed his last name to Lauder. The two became business partners, launching their beauty-products company in 1946. Thirteen years later, they didn't have enough money to buy ads in glossy women's magazines, so Lauder returned to her free-sample strategy. She lured department store customers with the promise of a gift. One of the first of these freebies was a light-blue compact containing her "revolutionary pressed powder."

Lauder's gift for promotion made her an early "influencer." Her talent for coming up with catchy slogans and product names also helped her win customers. One of Lauder's early mottos was: "Telephone, Telegraph, Tell-A-Woman." She called her anti-aging beauty ointments and creams "jars of hope." Her granddaughter, Aerin Lauder, wrote: "If Estée were alive today, she would be all over channels like Instagram and Pinterest."

As the new company grew rapidly through the 1960s and 1970s, Lauder continued to use her tactic of customer rewards. In the 1970s, a $5 purchase would get you a free lipstick, a lip gloss, and a compact. Meanwhile, Lauder began to hobnob with international celebrities. She courted them—and turned them into ambassadors for her products—with more free samples. "Mrs. Lauder is

SPREADING THE WORD

Public relations, or PR, is the way organizations communicate with the public and the media. A person who works in PR promotes a company and its products by explaining what the company's goals are and how the products work, what is new about them, and why they are worth buying. PR representatives reach out to newspaper and magazine writers, TV reporters, talk show hosts, bloggers, and other members of the media to spread the word about a business or product. They also use social media to convince people that their company, product, or service is worth trying out.

such a nice person," the late Princess Grace of Monaco once told an interviewer. "I don't know her very well, but she keeps sending all these things."

Lauder's tactics built her a phenomenal fortune. Her company was valued at about $5 billion when it went public in 1995. By 2003, it had 21,500 employees and was worth an estimated $10 billion. Its products, sold under the brands of Estée Lauder, Clinique, Origins, Prescriptives, and Aramis, have been sold in more than 130 countries on five continents.

Lauder achieved her self-made success at a time when few women were prominent in business. She had a work ethic and belief in herself and her business that can be models for ambitious women everywhere. "I worked every day from nine, when I arrived to polish my jars, to six in the evening. I never lunched," she has said.

> "I HAVE NEVER WORKED A DAY IN MY LIFE WITHOUT SELLING. IF I BELIEVE IN SOMETHING, I SELL IT, AND I SELL IT HARD."

Lauder died in 2004, when she was in her late nineties. One year later, *Time* magazine included her as the only woman on its list of the 20 most influential business geniuses of the century.

BE THE BRAND

As an elementary school student in Boca Raton, Rachel Zietz played several sports, including tennis and basketball, before she fell in love with lacrosse. "It was a new sport in Florida, and I love doing unconventional things," she said. "Besides, it makes you have to think ahead, and it's a team sport, so you're working with other girls for a common goal."

Each day after school, she would practice in her backyard—until her parents said she had to stop. They didn't want her slamming her dirty lacrosse balls against the walls, and they worried she'd break a window. Instead, Rachel convinced them to buy her a goal net and a rebounder—a trampoline-like surface that allowed her to practice her catching and throwing. But to Rachel's annoyance, the equipment began to rust and fall apart after only two months.

She didn't just get frustrated though. She began thinking of how to solve the problem. In 2012, when she was just 12 years old, she enrolled in a 33-week after-school program called the Young Entrepreneurs Academy. She cooked up a plan to design, manufacture, and sell her own superior equipment. Thinking strategically, she discovered a domain name on sale for just $10 that captured her competitive spirit. She called her new company Gladiator Lacrosse.

"WHAT GIVES ME THE EDGE IS I'M AUTHENTIC."

Rachel spent the next two years in intensive research and development, or R&D. With a $30,000 loan from her parents, she wrote a business plan and hired professional designers. The designers helped her create thicker nets and metal structures that would last longer without tearing or breaking. She soon realized she could cut costs by dealing directly with her manufacturers in China, rather than going through a middleman, as other companies do. She'd figured out how to make better, less expensive products.

Rachel began selling equipment in 2013, the year before she started high school. "I'm ahead of the game," she said, "because of how much I know the industry."

In its first year, Gladiator Lacrosse sold $200,000 worth of goals and rebounders. Within five years, Rachel grew her product line to include more equipment and started offering clothing too. Her company was earning $2 million, selling its products online, at tournaments, and in large chain retail stores throughout the country.

Rachel's years of playing lacrosse helped her understand the business. The sport is one of the fastest-growing pastimes in the United States. Rachel says the market could reach $100 million per year, and she hopes to dominate it.

Rachel comes from an entrepreneurial family. Her father founded his own business—and so did her brother (when he was only 13). When Rachel was just 10 years old, the family began getting together to watch *Shark Tank*, the reality show where entrepreneurs pitch their ideas to investors.

In 2015, Rachel herself appeared on *Shark Tank* to make the case for her growing company in front of about 9 million television viewers.

She strode onto the stage carrying a lacrosse stick and wearing the green jersey of her high school team. Watching her wow the panel of judges, few people would have guessed how scared she had been to go on national TV. But she had worked hard to prepare herself, practicing her pitch over and over. She told the judges she was seeking $100,000 to help her continue to expand her business. They all responded with raves. "You are the brand. You play the game—it's so credible," said one potential investor. "When people look at which product to buy, they're going to buy from a player."

Despite their enthusiasm, however, none of the judges was willing to invest. They all had their reasons, from not knowing enough about the sport to believing Rachel didn't truly need their help. "Of course I was bummed," said Rachel. But once again, she quickly rebounded. She took pride in how well she had prepared for the pitch, and understood that the judges' refusal to invest didn't mean her company was not bound for more success.

And of course she was right. In 2016, Rachel was recognized as one of *Time* magazine's most influential teens, along with Sasha and Malia Obama. She continues to push herself and her company, working three to five hours a day, even while earning straight A's in high school. Meanwhile, she constantly looks for ways to improve her products. Her advice to kids like her is to never fear trying something new. "It doesn't take an expert to start something," she says. "Just try it! When you do something you love, it's so rewarding."

WRITING A BUSINESS PLAN

A business plan is a written description of your business—an important step in getting started. Are you offering a service? Or selling a product? Who will buy your service or products? How is your idea different or better than other similar companies? You'll answer all of these questions in your business plan. You'll also write out how much you think it will cost to start the business and keep it going.

Ayanna Howard

DO GOOD TO DO WELL

Imagine a perfect friend for a child with a brain injury or disorder, a compassionate pal who would never get bored or impatient. In Ayanna Howard's vision, that friend might be made of aluminum, plastic, and wires.

Howard is a professor at Georgia Tech. She is also the founder of Zyrobotics, which makes software for robots designed to help millions of American children with serious brain disorders. "They're playmates and exercise coaches," she said of the small humanoids and other robots she works with. The machines are designed to teach simple tasks, such as reaching up or grabbing things, by demonstrating them over and over again. These movements can be difficult for kids with brain injuries. When the children fail to get it right, the robots will tilt their heads down and look sad. When they succeed, their mechanical friends will pump their fists or break out in a dance.

"If you could have a human doing this with kids every day, you'd get equivalent results," Howard explained. "But the reality is most kids can only get to their clinics once a week. So we're fulfilling an unmet need, providing a resource and service that doesn't exist."

Howard first fell in love with robots as a middle school student who was smitten by the TV show *The Bionic Woman*. The show's main character was seriously injured while skydiving, but then was rebuilt as the world's first female cyborg. She became a superhero, fighting to save humans in danger by lifting cars, crushing steel in her hands, and deactivating bombs. "I wanted to build that creature," Howard recalled. "I was techy and totally fascinated with sci-fi, and I wanted to save the world."

By 1999, at the age of 27, she was working for NASA's Jet Propulsion Laboratory. There, Howard led a team of engineers developing robots for future missions to Mars. Nine years later, she won international attention for her SnoMote robots, which were used to study the impact of climate change on glaciers.

She founded Zyrobotics in 2013 with funding from the National Science Foundation. Her main goal was to create products for kids with disabilities. But she soon realized she'd need a bigger market to help her company survive. Toward that end, she tweaked the design of some of her software to make games for kids without disabilities. Over the next five years, Zyrobotics grew to have eight employees and a stream of new products. Howard estimates that there have been 400,000 downloads of her software.

STEM Storiez is one of Zyrobotics products for mainstream children. It is an interactive e-book for kids who are just starting to read. Howard hopes it will help make STEM subjects familiar and engaging to kids as early as possible. She dreams of convincing girls to share her enthusiasm for science. "There's no question that girls have the aptitude," she has said. "They just need to understand and appreciate how scientists can change people's lives for the better."

> **"I HAD NO IDEA HOW TO LAUNCH A COMPANY. I FOUND ONES I THOUGHT WERE GOOD ONLINE AND SAID, 'I SEE YOU STARTED A BUSINESS AND ARE SUCCESSFUL. WOULD YOU MIND TALKING WITH ME?'"**

Katharine Graham

EXCELLENCE LEADS TO SUCCESS

No one was more surprised when Katharine Graham became the first woman publisher of a major newspaper than Katharine Graham herself. But she saw no choice other than to take over her husband Phil Graham's job at *The Washington Post* when he died in 1963. Almost immediately, she began to remake the paper into a journalistic powerhouse.

"I cared so much about the paper and about keeping it in the family that, despite my lack of knowledge and feelings of insecurity, I felt I had to make it work," she wrote in her autobiography, *Personal History*. "And so I got down to the job."

Graham had studied journalism in college and worked briefly as a reporter. But she had no time to study business or work her way up to the top of the corporation. All her training had to be on the job.

In the early 1970s, *The Washington Post* published stories about illegal activities involving President Richard Nixon. Investors worried that the *Post*'s negative stories about the president would bring down the company's earnings. Graham stood behind her reporters and editors and kept publishing the stories. She believed that reporting on the scandal known as Watergate was an important piece of the *Post*'s mission and that it would pay off.

She was right. The Watergate stories boosted profits. They

earned the *Post* a Pulitzer Prize, journalism's highest honor. And they led to President Nixon's resignation.

During her 30 years at the *Post*, perhaps the most important lesson Graham learned about running a news company was to focus on both turning out a first-rate publication and making money. "We operated under the philosophy," she wrote, "that journalistic excellence and profitability go hand in hand."

Under Graham's reign, the company's profits surged. At the same time, the newspaper transformed American journalism and the nation.

Graham had coined her phrase about excellence and profitability to signal to Wall Street investors that she cared about making money. "I wanted badly to answer the question of why anyone would invest in this company. I had to try to assure Wall Street that I wasn't some madwoman," she wrote, "but that I was also concerned with how we ran our business." She did her homework, hired the best and brightest editors, trusted them to do their jobs, and learned to follow her own sharp instincts.

> **"I BEGAN TO REALIZE THAT JUST BY PUTTING ONE FOOT IN FRONT OF THE OTHER I ACTUALLY WAS MOVING FORWARD."**

In her autobiography, Graham, who died in 2001, told the story of how she learned to be a chief executive while she was one. "I didn't understand the immensity of what lay before me, how frightened I would be by much of it, how tough it was going to be, and how many anxious hours and days I would spend for a long, long time," she wrote. "Nor did I realize how much I was eventually going to enjoy it all."

Julie Rice & Elizabeth Cutler

MAKE IT FUN

Daily exercise is good for you, as we all know. But not everyone does it. Some people think exercising is boring. Julie Rice and Elizabeth Cutler set out to solve that problem in 2006, when they launched SoulCycle.

The company offers 45-minute indoor fitness classes that combine stationary bike riding with dance moves and strength training. They look and feel like dance parties. In a dark, candlelit studio, you ride in a pack of cyclists, egged on by heart-pumping tunes and charismatic coaches.

The two founders joke that they "reinvented the wheel"—turning a dreaded chore into something people actually looked forward to. As Cutler put it: "The secret is a combination of endorphins, inspiration, and a sense of being part of something bigger than themselves—a community."

The two women were newcomers to New York City when they met over lunch. They were introduced by a mutual friend who knew they both were thinking about starting a new fitness business. Rice had spent 20 years as a talent scout in Hollywood. Cutler was a realtor. Both were new mothers looking for work that could be flexible and fun—and pay their bills.

They hit it off immediately, so much so that Cutler called Rice as they were heading home to say: "I'm going to look for real estate, and you should look for some towels." Six weeks later, they opened their first studio in an unlikely space: a former funeral parlor.

Worried relatives and friends asked them what they thought they were doing. In the conventional fitness business model, clients pay monthly fees to gyms that offer a variety of classes. SoulCycle had a different model. It charged for each class, a concept called "boutique fitness." The price was a hefty $27 for a ride. For that kind of money, the founders knew they had to offer something special.

The two had faith in their vision. They wrote out a business plan on a napkin at Starbucks. They figured out that they would need 100 riders a day to cover their costs, including babysitters for their own children. They soon surpassed that humble vision. In less than a decade, SoulCycle was reporting sales of $112 million from 75 studios. They had more than 2,000 employees and more than 20,000 riders per day.

> **"AS A SMALL BUSINESS, WE ARE NEVER TOO PROUD TO CHANGE, AND WE'RE ALSO ALWAYS TRYING TO EVOLVE."**
> —ELIZABETH CUTLER

It didn't hurt that SoulCycle became an instant hit with hip, bicoastal celebrities. Lena Dunham, Chelsea Clinton, Lady Gaga, Bradley Cooper, Beyoncé, and even Michelle Obama showed up for rides. Still, while SoulCycle's success may have looked easy from the outside, Rice and Cutler recall pounding the pavement with their strollers, handing out SoulCycle T-shirts and fliers. They spent years working behind the studio counters, checking in clients, and handing out special cycling shoes.

As both of them hoped, their entrepreneurial work combined well with their new lives as multitasking mothers. They could work long hours and also fix afternoon snacks and chaperone school field trips. They both learned to be expert delegators, meaning they passed on tasks to others so they didn't have to do everything themselves.

A large part of SoulCycle's magic comes from its rock-star instructors. New teachers must ace seriously competitive auditions and take ten weeks of full-time classes. They also get critiqued by more experienced instructors. "We're always looking for someone who has that 'it' factor," Cutler said. "Someone who's not only going to make you ride harder and faster but who you'd want to have dinner with and get to know."

The payback for instructors comes with great working conditions, including a good salary, health insurance, a clothing allowance, and even on-site physical therapists. Cutler said SoulCycle developed a culture of caring from its many years of majority-female leadership. "We operate much more like a galaxy than a pyramid," she explained. "We all have a lot to learn from each other."

In 2011, Rice and Cutler sold most of their stake in SoulCycle to Equinox, a big national fitness chain, to help them scale up. Five years later, they each felt it was time to move on, so they sold the rest and resigned. They continue to work together to advise and invest in other entrepreneurs.

> **"WE'RE ALWAYS LOOKING AT THINGS THROUGH THE EYES OF THE CONSUMER."**
> —JULIE RICE

Francesca Kennedy

BUILD A NETWORK

Francesca Kennedy spent summers swimming in Lake Atitlan in Guatemala, where her grandparents lived and her parents were born. When she returned to the lake in 2011, blue-green algae covered the water. It looked like sewage.

"I actually saw these little girls collecting water—to drink, to cook, to clean," she said. "It was an image that will stay with me for the rest of my life." More people die from drinking contaminated water than in wars, Kennedy said. She was determined to find a way to try to get the children clean water. That's when she conceived of Ix Style. *Ix* is the Mayan word for *water*. From the beginning, Ix Style has had a triple mission. It sells sandals, creates jobs for Guatemalan women, and provides clean drinking-water filters to their communities.

Kennedy quit her high-paying job at investment banking giant Goldman Sachs to work full time at Ix Style. By 2016, the company needed capital to manufacture sandals called huaraches. Latin Americans have been weaving together strips of leather to make huarache sandals for hundreds of years. Kennedy designed a modern version of the shoe to appeal to women today. She didn't know how to raise the necessary money, but she was convinced she could if she kept sharing her story.

She wrote in her journal: "I really want successful women to reach out to me out of the blue and help me with Ix Style." Sure enough, a few days later someone did. Kennedy was speaking on a panel about being a woman business owner. Another panelist, Alexandra Wilkis Wilson, had just been asked to be a judge on *Project Runway: Fashion Startup*. Entrepreneurs go on the show to pitch their product ideas to fashion and beauty executives. If the judges like the idea, they might invest money in the business in exchange for later profit.

Wilson, impressed with Kennedy, recommended that *Project Runway* give her a chance to make her case for investing in Ix Style. Presto! Kennedy was scheduled to be on national television to sell four potential investors a piece of her company.

If that wasn't enough, Kennedy's networking magic continued. Two days before she appeared on the show, she went to a party. She was, as always, wearing Ix sandals. Another partygoer complimented the shoes. Naturally, Kennedy told her about Ix Style and her passion for Guatemala. Kennedy's new friend, it just happened, knew fashion designer Rebecca Minkoff. Minkoff was one of the *Project Runway* judges Kennedy was about to meet.

Kennedy appeared nervous yet confident as she stood before the four judges and described the heartbreaking scene she had witnessed at Lake Atitlan.

Minkoff smiled encouragingly. Kennedy felt such an instant connection with her that she was sure her friend from the party had sung her praises.

When she saw young girls collecting dirty lake water, Kennedy told the judges, "I knew

> **BUILD YOUR NETWORK**
>
> When you're a kid, you make friends at school, on sports teams, and around your neighborhood. When you're in the working world, your circle grows to include people you work with and friends of friends. Your *network* of friends and colleagues can be helpful in many ways. You can share information, learn from each other, and meet more people. And, if you realize you need a photographer or a web designer for a project, you can reach out to people in your network for recommendations.

in that moment I wanted to do something to help them. So I went to the local market, and I saw the artisans making these beautiful huarache sandals, and a bell went off in my head. Why don't I update the style, create jobs for the artisans, as well as donate a percentage of the sales to provide clean drinking water for the children nearby?"

"Wow," Minkoff exclaimed.

Kennedy described herself as a "one-woman show," doing everything from public relations to sales to customer service. "Imagine what I could do with a little funding," she said. She asked for $300,000 in exchange for 10 percent of her company. "I'm asking you to invest in the change you want to see in the world."

Minkoff seemed riveted. "Funny story," she told Kennedy, "I actually received a pair of your shoes in a gift bag from an event. And I love them. They're the most comfortable shoes. I wear them all the time." Minkoff's enthusiasm set off a bidding war among her and two of the other judges. Each pledged a $50,000 investment in Ix Style.

Kennedy's lessons? First, always wear your product. Second, send out promotional gifts, like the shoes that wound up on Minkoff's feet. Third, know the key players in your industry. And, of course, always be ready to share your story.

"I can't emphasize this enough," she said. "You never know when you're going to run into someone and have an opportunity to share your brand's mission."

> **"IF YOU ARE CREATING A BUSINESS FOR THE RIGHT REASONS— WITH PURPOSE AND PASSION— YOUR CUSTOMERS WILL FEEL YOUR AUTHENTICITY AND SHARE YOUR STORY AND PROMOTE AND HELP YOUR CAUSE."**

Rosanna Pansino

BE **CHOOSY**

Apple Pi Pie. Dinosaur Fossil Cookies. Mermaid Tail Cupcakes. These are just a few of the "Nerdy Nummies" that helped snag more than 2 billion cumulative views for Rosanna Pansino's YouTube channel.

The bubbly star, who goes by Ro and loves corny puns, came up with the recipe for her baking show in 2011. At the time, she was in her twenties and sleeping on a couch in an apartment with six roommates in Los Angeles, where she was working as an extra on *Glee*. She shot her early videos on an $80 Flip Video camera and edited them herself. She wasn't making any money from her videos, but she loved what she was doing, and her audience was growing. She decided to invest her life savings—about $20,000—in better equipment, including baking supplies, professional lighting, and a better editing program.

It turned out to be a smart bet. In addition to having nearly 10 million subscribers, Pansino comes across as warm and likable, an approach that has drawn interest from many potential sponsors. Still, she says she turns down more than 90 percent of the offers she gets. Having spent more than a year producing videos without earning a dime, it's clear that money is not her primary motivation.

"Whenever I decide to partner with a brand, it has to be a brand that I absolutely love and I use in real life," she has said. Pansino knows that her authenticity—a genuine passion for baking and the geeky characters she re-creates in dessert form—is what resonates with her fans. In the first episode of Nerdy Nummies, she made a Super Mario star-shaped cake to share with a bunch of friends—because *that's* what she loves to do. She used Wilton icing and fondant on that first cake. Later, when she was ready to launch a signature line of bakeware, it was only fitting that she would partner with a beloved brand: Wilton.

She has also worked with Disney, Nintendo, Barbie, Hasbro, and many others.

Pansino is just as choosy about her employees as she is about her brand partnerships: Her small production team includes her sister, mother, and father. At the office and through YouTube, Pansino has fostered a strong sense of community. Millions of fans look forward to viewing her newest release every Tuesday. Her fans also helped turn her 2015 cookbook into a best-seller.

"I always believed in the YouTube community and myself," she said. Pansino's faith was tested long before her YouTube channel took off. When her former agent said she had to choose between her acting career and YouTube business, she went with what she was most passionate about. Now she's one of the highest-earning women on YouTube—bringing in as much as $6 million a year. Smart move.

A BRAND IS MORE THAN A NAME

What is a brand? It's a name for a product made by a particular company. For example, Dove, Dial, and Irish Spring are brands of soap. Ben & Jerry's, Häagen-Dazs, and Turkey Hill are brands of ice cream. Customers recognize brands by their names, colors, logos, and slogans. But a successful brand is much more than that. A successful brand stands for everything people think of when they picture a particular brand. When someone thinks of the DVF signature wrap dress, she may think of simple elegance and confidence. When someone thinks of Nerdy Nummies, she may think of bright, cheerful time spent in the kitchen and sharing fun geek-chic treats with her friends. Companies show off their branding in their ads, commercials, partnerships, packaging, logos, and website design.

Pleasant Rowland

MARKET **DIRECTLY** TO YOUR CUSTOMERS

While shopping for Christmas gifts in the 1980s, Pleasant Rowland discovered a gaping hole in the doll aisle. She was looking for a doll who resembled her nieces, ages 8 and 10. All she could find were baby dolls, Barbies, and Cabbage Patch Kids. "To put it nicely," she said, she was "dismayed" by the "pitiful" selection.

At around the same time, Rowland had visited Colonial Williamsburg, in Virginia. She sat in the pew where President George Washington attended church and stood at the podium where Virginia governor Patrick Henry spoke. "I remember sitting on a bench in the shade, reflecting on what a poor job schools do of teaching history, and how sad it was that more kids couldn't visit this fabulous classroom of living history," she said. "Was there some way I could bring history alive for them, the way Williamsburg had for me?"

There was. Rowland had been a teacher and a textbook writer. She was thinking about the need for real-looking dolls and ways to engage children in history when she dreamed up her girls—Molly McIntire, Samantha Parkington, and Kirsten Larson.

Kirsten was a Swedish immigrant living on the American frontier in 1854. Samantha was an orphan adopted by wealthy grandparents in 1904. And Molly lived during World War II. These were the American Girl dolls that every girl would want.

Rowland had saved more than $1 million from her publishing career. She invested it in Pleasant Company. In 18 months, it manufactured the three dolls, published nine novels recounting the American Girls' stories, and produced a line of doll clothing and accessories. The dolls would prompt the girls to read about history and, with them, act it out.

The most challenging question was how to introduce the dolls to children. Toy stores told her that, at $82 a doll, the American Girls were too expensive to stock.

> **"READING IS AT THE HEART OF ALL ACHIEVEMENT."**

"It was clear to me that American Girl was a thinking girl's product line, one that would not sell at Toys 'R' Us," Rowland told *CNN Money*. "It wasn't meant to blare from the shelves on its packaging or visual appeal alone. It had a more important message—one that had to be delivered in a softer voice."

That voice came in the form of a catalog with photographs of the dolls mailed to girls' homes. Directly mailing catalogs to the homes of potential customers was becoming a common way to sell products in the 1980s. Rowland hired a company to create an address list. The company recommended sending out no more than 100,000 catalogs. "No way," said Rowland. "We had to take our shot that Christmas, and American Girl would either succeed or fail. So we mailed 500,000 catalogs and crossed our fingers."

Rowland bet on her intuition and direct mail—and won. Sales of American Girl dolls and merchandise hit $50 million by 1990 and kept climbing. Revenue peaked at $300 million in 1998, when Rowland sold the company to Mattel for $700 million.

Now that's the dream of an American girl.

Jessica Alba

LEARN ON THE JOB

Jessica Alba's business was born while she was pregnant with her first child. Alba was prewashing her baby's cloth diapers when she broke out in hives and start sneezing. The detergent she was using was supposed to be safe for newborns. "If this is how my skin reacts, there is no way I am putting this on my newborn!" she thought.

Alba, most famous for her role as a superhuman soldier on the TV show *Dark Angel*, is all too familiar with the dangers of common chemicals. As a child, she suffered from severe asthma and allergies. Over time, she realized that certain products, like detergents or hairspray, routinely made her feel worse, causing headaches, wheezing, and rashes. She didn't want her child to suffer similar reactions, and she knew she wasn't the only mother (or expectant mother) to feel that way.

In 2012, Alba launched The Honest Company with 17 products, including detergent and diapers, all made with natural ingredients. Its mission is to "empower people to live happy, healthy lives," by creating safe products.

At first Alba had to work to find willing investors. "Everyone I approached was skeptical," she told one interviewer. The criticisms felt all too familiar. From the age of 12, she has said, she had been told "I wasn't good enough; I was too 'Latin'; I wasn't 'Latin' enough; I was too exotic to be a leading lady. I got the same thing when I started the business."

Alba had faith in her plan, however—and both her instincts and timing were excellent. In recent years, more and more consumers have been looking for products with safe, natural ingredients.

Alba was sure about the kind of company she wanted to build, but she also knew how much she had to learn. She hadn't been to business school and initially knew very little about the chemistry of the products she wanted to make. She made the wise decision to partner with experts who could advise her. And she did "deep dives of research" on her own. She knew how important it was to have the confidence to ask questions when she didn't know the answers. "I came from a completely other business, and I had to learn to embrace that instead of being embarrassed about it," she has said. "I just try to be productive and stay open and curious and always try to better myself."

In just a few years, The Honest Company had become a big success. Its stylishly packaged products were sold online and in big box stores like Target. By 2016, it employed hundreds of people and had expanded to include more than 500 products.

Like all businesses, the company has had some growing pains.

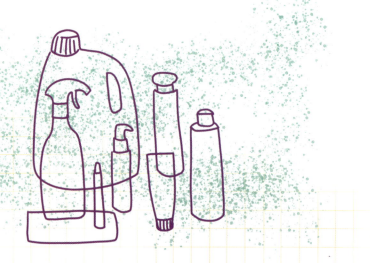

Some customers have questioned whether the products are truly safe and natural. Alba has had to be prepared to stand up for her products and their ingredients.

In 2017, The Honest Company got some great news. It was awarded the *Good Housekeeping* seal of approval for four of its cleaning products. The certification meant the products passed serious tests by people who didn't work for The Honest Company or for *Good Housekeeping* magazine. The seal also included a customer warranty—a promise that *Good Housekeeping* would pay a customer back if the product didn't work.

In addition to creating products that don't contain harsh chemicals, The Honest Company donates goods to people in need. As of January 2018, it had given away 15 million products and employees had spent more 15,000 hours helping others through the Honest to Goodness program.

Alba's interest in natural products isn't limited to her company. As she learned more about the common chemicals used in everyday products, she also traveled to Washington, D.C., to ask lawmakers to strengthen regulations on them.

Alba is proud of her business career. "I am trying my hardest to make a difference in the world," she says. "I try to learn from my mistakes. And I try to live an honest life."

> **"PARTNER WITH PEOPLE WHO ARE SMARTER THAN YOU, UNDERSTAND YOUR STRENGTHS AND WEAKNESSES, AND SURROUND YOURSELF WITH PEOPLE WHO COMPLEMENT YOUR STRENGTHS BUT COULD SUPPORT YOUR WEAKNESSES."**

DO IT **YOURSELF**

Limor Fried was procrastinating. She was avoiding the work she should have been doing as an MIT graduate student by doing what she loves—making things. She made video games and built an MP3 music player in an Altoids box. She'd post pictures of her projects on her website, and she'd get email requests for "kits" with the materials and instructions for making them.

At the time, in 2005, the concept of open-source software—or sharing technology so that the world could benefit from it—was taking off. "I was just soaking in this idea that if you are creating new technology, new capabilities, you have to give it away," Fried said. "Otherwise you're kind of being selfish."

Fried wanted to share her secrets. She thought of the materials and instructions for her do-it-yourself, or DIY, projects as "open-source hardware." From her dorm room, she began designing and selling user-friendly starter electronic kits.

Her customers knew her as LadyAda. Ada Lovelace, a British mathematician who wrote instructions for the first computer program in the 1800s, inspired the name.

In 2006, at 27, Fried moved to New York City and started her company, Adafruit, out of her apartment. Adafruit manufactures kits to help people of all ages learn about electronics and engineering.

For example, it sells a kit to activate lights on your bow tie, a kit to light your sneakers when you walk, and a kit to build a remote control to shut off any television within 300 feet.

"Electronics engineering for me is my art form," Fried said. "What I'm trying to do is inspire people to become curious and practice using technology." She aims to give them the tools to build anything they might imagine.

More than 100 people work at Adafruit. It operates out of 50,000 square feet—that's 25 times the size of a large suburban house—in the middle of Manhattan, one of the priciest cities on the planet. Robots, eyeballs, glowing costumes, and boxes of kits fill the factory.

Adafruit is among the top 25 private manufacturing companies in the United States. By 2018, it had sold more than 1.7 million DIY kits and built one of the biggest collections of free electronic tutorial videos on the internet. It had also made more than $45 million a year in revenue.

Though Adafruit stresses the importance of community, the company's focus is all about learning to do it yourself. Fried, the first woman engineer featured on the cover of *Wired* magazine, has earned the nickname "DIY Goddess." And she's built the business on her own—without any loans or investors. All the risk, all the headaches, and all the profit are Adafruit's alone.

BUILDING COMMUNITY

A pink-haired electrical engineer, Limor Fried sees connecting her community of customers to one another as key to Adafruit's success. The company hosts a weekly live "show-and-tell" program for fans, hobbyists, and crafters to stop by and share what they're making.

"It used to be just freaks in garages." Fried has said. "Now it's freaks in garages working together."

One of the highlights of Fried's career came when she received a note from a man who had watched her show-and-tell program with his daughter. When it was over, the girl turned to him and said, "Wow, this is so cool." Then she asked: "Can boys be engineers too?"

"We're not against investment or loans. We just have not needed them," Fried said. Having no financial safety net can be challenging at times. "But," she said, "maybe that makes us consider things more carefully and make better decisions." Not taking money from outside investors has allowed Fried to take chances without the pressure of having to explain what she's doing to anyone outside the company. Not relying on other people's money has allowed Adafruit to grow more slowly and more organically, because Fried didn't have investors rushing her to make greater profits.

Being independent has allowed Fried to create her business on her own terms. The DIY Goddess wouldn't have it any other way.

> "YOU DON'T HAVE TO BE ORIGINAL. ORIGINALITY COMES LATER, AFTER YOU'VE GAINED SKILL WITH THE MATERIAL."

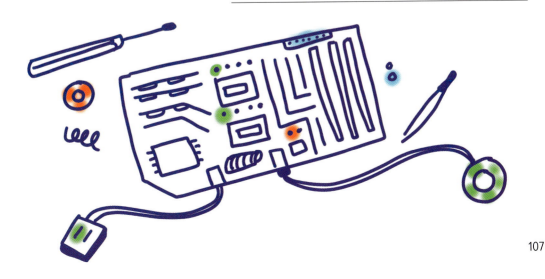

KNOW YOUR CUSTOMERS

As a child, Venus Williams began preparing for two careers. While her father drove her and her younger sister, Serena, to tennis matches, Venus listened to books on tape about how to make money in real estate. At the same time she dreamed of becoming a tennis star, she also dreamed of becoming an entrepreneur. Her father, Richard Williams, saw tennis as his daughters' best shot at opportunities rarely available to African-American girls. He taught them how to play the game after figuring it out himself by studying videos and reading books.

In 1990, when she was 10, Williams' serve was faster than 100 miles an hour, and she was winning every tournament. By 14, she turned pro. She had pushed beyond the limits of what was expected of a girl who learned to serve on the rough public tennis courts of East Compton Park in Southern California.

By 20, she was six foot one and the winner of three major singles competitions: Wimbledon, the U.S. Open, and the 2000 Summer Olympics. She also had a $40 million endorsement deal from Reebok. It was the largest deal a female athlete had ever signed. Under the five-year contract, she wore Reebok sneakers and a "Venus" line of clothing. Trading "tennis whites" for bright, patterned outfits, Williams' playful style changed the way women dressed on the court.

After studying fashion design, she decided to create her own line of active wear. In 2007, she started EleVen. It makes women's tennis outfits and workout clothes. The name came from the Williams family's first home in California. It also has another meaning. "EleVen stands for being better than a ten," Williams said. "It's about reaching your best, pushing beyond the limits, and coming to win. Even if you don't get there, it's about that journey."

Williams is the face of her brand. She wears her clothing and lives a life reflecting the brand's message: being your absolute best. Although she was diagnosed with Sjogren's syndrome, a disease that makes her tired and achy, she continues to work out five or six hours a day and to compete around the world.

Not your average company executive, Williams often shows up to business meetings sweaty from her workout. Once, in a meeting with EleVen's ad agency, she pointed out that the models in the photos looked too perfect in her clothes. To Williams, they did not look authentic. She designs for active, athletic women and wanted to see ads showing them sweating with their ponytails messy after working out, she explained. She wanted to see women like herself and her customers in her ads.

Williams could have relied on her fame alone to launch her brand. Instead, she earned degrees in fashion design and business administration. She serves as EleVen's lead designer, sketches nearly every item the brand develops, and tries on samples when they arrive from the factory. And she's the CEO.

WANT TO RUN A BUSINESS? PLAY A SPORT.

A recent study looked at the backgrounds of 400 female executives in five countries. It found that more than half (52 percent) of the C-suite level executives (that means they are CEO, CFO, COO, or on the board of directors of a company) played a sport at the college or university level. Only 3 percent of the execs did not play sports at any point in their lives. Playing sports encourages competitiveness, teamwork, hard work, determination, and discipline—all traits that help people get ahead in business.

Williams is one of the most recognized people in the sports world. But that didn't make launching a business easy. In 2007, she signed an exclusive deal with a chain of stores. Under the agreement, the chain would manufacture the EleVen line, and only it could sell the clothing. But the chain went out of business, and Williams had to start from scratch. "Being an entrepreneur is about having a dream and finding the path to it," she said. "The path is not always straight."

After that detour, Williams struggled to put together the right team and the right business model. As someone who was used to pounding balls over the net again and again, she was determined to see her business dream materialize. In 2015, she restructured EleVen, focusing on her own and the company's strengths. That's when she hit her stride.

In 2016, she described EleVen customers to *Vogue* magazine. "They are the dreamers and the doers," she said. "The focused and the hungry. . . . The women who aspire to accomplish whatever goals and dreams they set their minds to. The self-assured who are ready to take on any and *all* challenges that come their way."

Williams is an 11.

> **"MY BEST ADVICE FOR STAYING FOCUSED AND POSITIVE DURING STRESSFUL TIMES IS TO REALIZE THAT THOSE TIMES DON'T LAST FOREVER."**

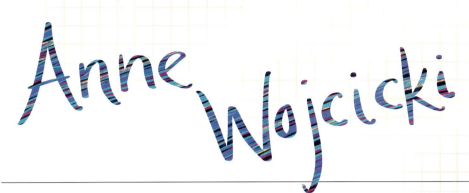

SETBACKS ARE **OPPORTUNITIES** TO LEARN

How much do you really want to know about yourself? Are you curious about where your ancestors are from? Would you want to know whether you're at risk of a serious disease?

Anne Wojcicki founded 23andMe on the assumption that you'll want to know a lot. Information, she says, is key to a lifetime of making smart decisions to protect your health.

Wojcicki was 33 years old in 2006, when, together with two colleagues, she launched her company. She named it after the 23 pairs of chromosomes that contain our genetic code, or DNA. More than 5 million people have since signed up as customers. Meanwhile, Wojcicki has faced setbacks that have earned her fame as the tech industry's comeback kid.

The premise of her company is simple. For $199, you receive a little vial, which you spit into and mail back. Wait another two months, and you'll get reports on your health and ancestry. You'll find out, for instance, if you have a high chance of developing breast cancer, Alzheimer's disease, or a condition that makes it more likely that you'll suffer from blood clots. You may also learn you have Latino or Scandinavian ancestors you never knew about before. Some people have even discovered long-lost living relatives.

"The beauty of it is we all have so much genetic information in common; we're actually all very similar," said Wojcicki. "There are really just some tiny differences between us, which mostly come from our environment and how we've been raised."

If you're under 18, you'll need a parent's permission to sign up for the tests. Then, whatever your age, you can use the information to make healthy decisions. If you're at high risk for breast cancer, you can take steps to reduce the chance you'll actually get the disease, including keeping your weight down and getting plenty of exercise.

Back when 23andMe was getting started, some people were paying hundreds of thousands of dollars for this kind of information, and they could only get it from doctors. But that's not the only reason Wojcicki believes her company is revolutionizing health care. She also asks customers if they would like to contribute their information to researchers seeking new treatments for illnesses that tend to run in families, such as depression and Parkinson's disease.

Wojcicki, who studied biology at Yale, worked for a decade as a health-care investor on Wall Street before deciding she wanted to do more with her life than make money.

Her new business was an almost instant success. In 2008, *Time* magazine called Wojcicki's test kit the "Invention of the Year." By 2013, her company was on its way to becoming a "unicorn": a start-up company valued at $1 billion or more.

But that's when she ran into those setbacks. The U.S. Food and Drug Administration (FDA) declared Wojcicki's little vial to be an "unapproved medical device" and suspended its use for health testing purposes, though they did allow her to continue using it for ancestry information.

"Sure, I was distraught," Wojcicki said. "Someone even told me this is when companies typically fold." But closing down never occurred to her. "I'm the kind of person who is rarely deterred," she said.

She learned this approach from her mother, Esther, a high school teacher. The child of Russian immigrants, Esther was the first in her family to attend college. "She's a fighter," Wojcicki explained. "She has always said it doesn't matter what happened today—make it better tomorrow."

Wojcicki hired experts in government regulations, spent hours on the phone with lawyers, and improved her company's communications with consumers. She also compiled data proving that 23andMe's testing was accurate and that the average consumer could understand the genetic information. Wojcicki's efforts paid off. The government lifted its ban.

"Setbacks and controversies aren't necessarily a bad thing," Wojcicki said. "In this case, we ended up being defined as a company willing to persevere. The takeaway is that as an entrepreneur, you have to be persistent. Then every experience you have ends up being valuable."

> **"IF SOMEONE SAYS 'NO' TO ME, I SAY: 'WHY?'"**

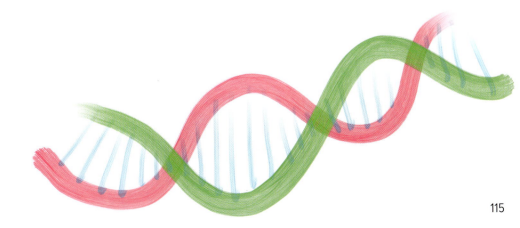

J.K. Rowling

KEEP CONTROL OF YOUR BRAND

J.K. Rowling is not a CEO. She is a hugely successful author, famous for her fantasy stories about wizards who cast spells and fly on broomsticks. Still, when it comes to business, she is also a legend for making careful, savvy decisions.

Her Harry Potter series has sold more than 500 million copies in 70 languages. The movies based on her stories have earned more than $7 billion. There is even a popular Florida theme park based on her work. Rowling is not only the creative genius behind these ventures but is also responsible for a good deal of financial wizardry.

Rowling's personal story is packed with its own drama. She famously wrote the first draft of her future blockbuster in coffee shops while her infant daughter napped. At the time, she was a divorced and depressed single mother receiving government benefits. She was "as poor as it is possible to be in modern Britain, without being homeless," she has said. Twelve publishers turned down the manuscript before one finally paid her a relatively small advance. Even then, her editor suggested that Rowling get a day job, since she'd never make much money as a children's author.

Harry Potter and the Philosopher's Stone was first published in Britain in 1997. (You may know it better as *Harry Potter and the Sorcerer's Stone*, the title used in the United States.) Since then, Rowling has made a series of bold decisions that led to her becoming the world's first billionaire author. But making money was not her priority.

"Once you've made a lot of money, people around you might be full of ideas about ways to make lots more money and might be disappointed that you don't want to seize every opportunity to do so," she has said. But Rowling made sure to guard her creation. She turned down a proposal for a McDonald's Harry Potter Happy Meal, among other lucrative licensing opportunities. And she made sure that the Warner Bros. film adaptations of the Harry Potter series stayed faithful to her books.

One of her smartest moves was to retain all ebook rights to her books. Typically, publishers will control the rights to both printed books and ebooks, but Rowling insisted on keeping her ebook rights. That decision gave her complete control over how her ebooks would be sold.

In 2012, Rowling launched Pottermore, a website full of news, features, and her new writing. It fostered community for her fans—another wise move. For a short time, it was also the only site where fans could buy Harry Potter ebooks and digital audio books. Selling directly to her fans allowed Rowling to cut the bookstore out of the equation. (She opted to give her print publishers a share of ebook revenues, although she was not obligated to do so.)

Rowling's smart business decisions have given her the freedom to keep challenging herself. After finishing the Harry Potter series, she ventured into screenwriting, producing, and authoring three adult

> **"THE DISCIPLINE INVOLVED IN FINISHING A PIECE OF CREATIVE WORK IS SOMETHING ON WHICH YOU CAN TRULY PRIDE YOURSELF."**

novels under a pseudonym, or pen name. "You sort of start thinking anything's possible if you've got enough nerve," she has said.

In 2012, Rowling dropped off the *Forbes* list of billionaires, in part because she'd given so much of her money away. "I think you have a moral responsibility, when you've been given far more than you need, to do wise things with it and give intelligently," she has said. She has contributed money to help women and children in poverty and to support research on multiple sclerosis, a disease her mother suffered from. In 2005, she launched her own international charity, Lumos. Named after the light-giving spell in the Harry Potter books, the organization works to help the millions of children in orphanages worldwide.

Rowling has spoken about what she learned from hitting bottom just before she wrote her first Potter book. In a graduation speech at Harvard on the "benefits of failure," she described her early struggles as having helped her direct her energy into finishing "the only work that mattered to me." She said, "Had I really succeeded at anything else, I might never have found the determination to succeed in the one arena I believed I truly belonged. I was set free, because my greatest fear had already been realized, and I was still alive, and I still had a daughter whom I adored, and I had an old typewriter and a big idea. And so rock bottom became the solid foundation on which I rebuilt my life."

HOW DO AUTHORS MAKE MONEY?

J.K. Rowling's runaway publishing success is unique. But other authors can also make money, even if their books aren't turned into movies and theme parks. If you write a great book and a publisher decides to publish it, you will be paid an advance against royalties. This means that they give you a fixed amount of money up front. A percentage of the price of each book sold (a royalty) is then credited to you until the advance "earns out." Once the publisher is paid back for the advance, you will begin to receive payment for your royalties. You can also earn money if foreign publishers want to make an edition of your book—or if somebody wants to adapt it into a film.

Mary Barra

DO THE **RIGHT** THING

Two months after Mary Barra took over as General Motors' chief executive, she faced a crisis. GM recalled millions of cars because of a defective ignition switch linked to at least 124 deaths and numerous serious injuries. As part of the recall, the company had to contact each of the car owners and arrange to repair the vehicles for free. Barra—the first woman to lead a major car manufacturer—confronted a flood of criminal and congressional investigations, lawsuits, and anguish from the families whose loved ones died in faulty GM cars.

Many CEOs would have tried to minimize the problem. Not Barra. She'd worked herself up from the factory floor to the top of the nation's biggest automaker. GM was her company, and she insisted on meeting the challenge head on.

"We want to do the right thing," she said as the legal consequences from the defective switch started to become clear in 2014. "I never want to put this behind us. I want to keep this painful experience in our collective memories."

At a time when other CEOs might have gone into hiding, Barra met with the grieving parents. She apologized to each parent, one after another. She did something CEOs rarely do in public. She wiped tears from her eyes.

Barra promised the relatives she'd search for the truth about what happened to their children. Not only is Barra the chief executive of an enormous company, but she's also a mother. "I put myself in their shoes and thought they deserved to be heard," Barra told *Forbes* magazine. "It was very difficult for them, and I think they needed to know that General Motors cared and that we listened."

She took responsibility and committed herself and her company to doing the right thing. She authorized an investigation to figure out how the defective switches wound up in the cars and why it took so long to get them out. She instituted a policy called "Speak Up For Safety" and pledged "when we find a problem, we're going to fix it."

Barra grew up at GM. Her father worked at the company's Pontiac factory for 39 years. He was a die maker, creating molds for the exteriors of vehicles. She spent the summer she was 18 inspecting hood and fender panels at a Pontiac plant. Then she earned an electrical engineering degree from GMI Engineering & Management Institute, which was owned by the company at the time and is now known as Kettering University. A GM fellowship paid for her to attend Stanford University, where she earned a master's degree in business administration.

There were no women engineers or executives in the auto industry in 1961, the year Barra was born. Early on in her career, one

assembly-line worker whistled whenever she passed. Finally, Barra asked the whistler what he was doing. He wanted her attention, he replied. She suggested he could accomplish his goal by saying "hi." The whistling stopped.

"I have this fundamental belief that everybody is pretty rational," she said. "If you can understand what is motivating them or change what is motivating them, you can accomplish things."

In 2015, *Fortune* magazine rated her the most powerful woman in business. The following year, GM's board of directors elected her board chair. Chairing the board and being the CEO makes Barra one of the most influential people in American business today.

She plans to use her influence to power a world filled with all-electric, driverless cars. "We're working toward a goal with zero crashes, zero emissions, and zero congestion," she said. "I think it's important for the world."

> **"WHEN YOU SOLVE ISSUES FOR WOMEN, YOU SOLVE ISSUES FOR EVERYONE."**

THE GLASS CEILING

Have you heard about the glass ceiling? It refers to an invisible barrier that stops women from advancing to upper-level positions even if they are qualified. Instead of breaking through a glass ceiling, Sheryl Sandberg, Facebook's chief operating officer, described Mary Barra's promotion to CEO of GM as smashing the "steel ceiling."

Madam C.J. Walker

GROW A **GRASSROOTS** SALES FORCE

Decades before Sarah Breedlove made history as the first self-made black female millionaire, she was the daughter of newly freed slaves, growing up in poverty on a cotton plantation near Delta, Louisiana. She was orphaned at age 7, married at 14, and pregnant with her first child at 17. Her husband died a few years later. After that, Breedlove moved to St. Louis, Missouri, where her elder brothers were barbers. There, she worked as a low-paid washerwoman through most of the 1890s.

In those years, many African-American women suffered from scalp ailments that caused them to lose their hair. It was a humiliating predicament, and Breedlove herself wasn't spared. But with resilience and ingenuity, she bounced back to make it the source of her success.

Around 1905, when she was living in Denver and working as a pharmacist's cook, she learned some basic chemistry. She began to experiment with formulas to cure scalp troubles. Then she married a newspaper ad salesman named Charles Joseph Walker and reinvented herself as an entrepreneur named Madam C.J. Walker.

Walker was born in an era of tremendous opportunity. Railroads and telephone lines were expanding and hundreds of new factories were being built. At the same time, women were only just starting to be recognized as consumers. Other female entrepreneurs, including Elizabeth Arden and Helena Rubinstein, seized the moment, like Walker did, to reinvent themselves as elegant marketing geniuses.

Walker came up with powerful stories for her products. She told one reporter that the formula for her signature "Madam C.J. Walker's Wonderful Hair Grower" had come to her in a dream. "A big black man appeared to me and told me what to mix up for my hair," she said. "Some of the remedy was grown in Africa, but I sent for it, mixed it, put it on my scalp, and in a few weeks my hair was coming in faster than it had ever fallen out. I tried it on my friends; it helped them. I made up my mind I would begin to sell it."

At the time, she reportedly had just $1.25 in capital. (Capital is the money, materials, or products used to start or run a business.) But, like any good entrepreneur, Walker started out small. She also leaned on her network. At first, she sold her Wonderful Hair Grower, Glossine, and Vegetable Shampoo at her church. Later she expanded to other churches throughout the South.

As part of a particularly effective strategy, Walker trained many of her first customers to be door-to-door saleswomen, following a business model that had been recently pioneered by the famous Avon ladies. Walker called her saleswomen "Walker Agents," and

"I GOT MY START BY GIVING MYSELF A START."

devoted herself to improving their lives. "I am not satisfied in making money for myself," she said. "I endeavor to provide employment for hundreds of the women of my race." Many of her thousands of agents would otherwise have been working as maids or cooks. Walker trained them not only to win over customers, but to set up shop in their homes and keep business records.

As Walker became older and wealthier, her influence grew. She campaigned against the attacks, known as "lynchings," in which mobs murdered African-Americans. She also spoke up for better treatment of black soldiers who served in the U.S. military.

By 1910, Walker was earning the modern-day equivalent of millions of dollars a year from her hair products. She set up headquarters in Indianapolis and expanded internationally to the Caribbean and Central America. By the time she died, in 1919, at the age of 51, she had trained as many as 40,000 Walker agents. Her message to them was: Do not wait for opportunities to be handed to you. "Get up and make them!" she said.

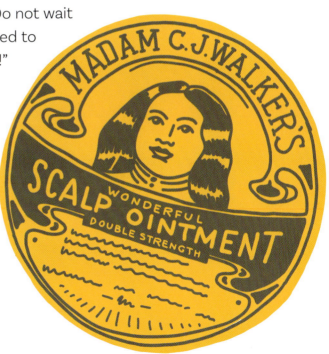

Heidi Ganahl

BUILD A FRANCHISE

Heidi Ganahl owned two Colorado doggy daycare and boarding facilities called Camp Bow Wow when a sales director for Mrs. Fields, the cookie company, arrived with his dog. He looked around and asked: "Have you ever thought about franchising this?" Starting a franchise is like cloning a business. Each business is independently owned and operated, but it looks and acts just like all the others.

When Ganahl first researched it in 2003, no one had franchised a dog care facility. She learned that if she started a Camp Bow Wow franchise, people who bought the right to open a camp would pay her an upfront fee and a percentage of the sales income.

After investigating the pros and cons of franchises, Ganahl put a sign on the counter of both of her camps asking if anyone would like to open a Camp Bow Wow. In the first year and a half, she sold 15.

"It was a lot of fun to see other people see their dreams of owning their own business come true," she said. As the franchise owner, she helped people who bought a Camp Bow Wow understand zoning laws so they could figure out where they could open. She helped franchisees, or the people who bought franchises, hire contractors to build kennels and animal runs. She helped them plan their grand openings and provided expertise on how to manage the business.

She told them about the mistakes she had made so they could avoid making them too. "The beauty of franchising only lies in the cohesiveness of everybody in the vision," she said. "If everybody's off doing their own thing, it doesn't work."

One day in 2005, Ganahl's phone began ringing off the hook. Thousands of people wanted to open Camp Bow Wow franchises. At first, Ganahl couldn't figure out what set off the sudden surge of interest. Then a friend told her that AOL, one of the first Internet providers, had featured Camp Bow Wow as "the next great franchise."

Within the next year, Ganahl sold about 75 more franchises. Her biggest challenge was screening applicants. "If they're too entrepreneurial and independent, it's hard to keep them aligned with using the right logo and vendors and systems," she said. "We put them through diligent screening processes and made sure they were in it for the right reasons."

Camp Bow Wow's success followed in the wake of tragedy. The idea for the business came to Ganahl and her first husband nine years earlier, in 1994, when they couldn't find a place they were comfortable leaving their two beloved dogs while they were at work or on vacation. They wrote out a plan for a doggy daycare business. It boiled down to "all day play, snooze the night away."

TIME TESTED, CUSTOMER APPROVED

One of the reasons that franchises have a high success rate is that the businesses have already been tested. When a franchisee buys a franchise, she knows that the business model has already worked in another location (and sometimes in many locations). She also knows that the name and look of the business will be familiar to customers.

Customers know what they can get before they even step through the door. Mrs. Fields is a franchise. So are Ben & Jerry's and Baskin-Robbins. When you walk into a Baskin-Robbins in Columbus, Ohio, it looks just like one in Atlanta, Georgia, or Seattle, Washington. The menu always looks the same, and the ice cream always tastes the same. Customers can count on it.

"A BUSINESS IS ONLY AS STRONG AS THE PEOPLE WHO RUN IT."

Five months after they conceived the idea, Ganahl's husband died in a small-plane crash. Ganahl was in no position to start a business. She had to figure out how to get out of bed. She won a $1 million settlement from the plane's insurance company. But she spent most of it quickly. She lent money to friends and family and used some of the settlement to start two companies that did not take off.

Five years after the fatal accident, Ganahl's brother suggested she dust off the plan for Camp Bow Wow. She took what little money she had left and opened the first camp in Denver in 2000.

Camp Bow Wow's motto was "don't put the dollar before the dog." It was a winner.

Ganahl sold the first franchise to a single woman in Colorado with two beagles for $20,000 and 5 percent of her sales. By 2014, there were 120 Camp Bow Wows, another 50 in line to become franchises, and another 50 in-home pet-sitting franchises. That's when VCA Inc. bought the entire Camp Bow Wow franchise for $20 million.

Franchising worked for Ganahl. "I didn't have enough money to open 200 locations," she said. "Franchising grows the brand."

Linda Alvarado

REDEFINE WOMEN'S WORK

Linda Alvarado likes to tell a story about what happened after she spoke to her son's kindergarten class for a career day. During the question-and-answer part, the teacher asked her son if he wanted to build schools and sports stadiums, like his mom, when he grew up.

"No," Alvarado's son piped up. "That's women's work!"

Alvarado has spent her adult life ignoring men who've tried to tell her what is or isn't women's work. It's how she got to be the founder and CEO of Alvarado Construction, one of the nation's most successful general contractors. Her company has offices in several states and has built multimillion dollar projects throughout the United States and Latin America.

Alvarado grew up in Albuquerque, New Mexico, the only girl in a low-income family of six children. Her mother encouraged her to defy stereotypes in playing sports and building tree houses with her brothers. She even supported her daughter's wish to attend Pomona College in California on a scholarship. Alvarado said that at that time it was "very non-traditional" for a Latina girl to go away to college. As a student, despite having been told by everyone that only boys would be hired, she still applied with a landscaping company and got a job as a groundskeeper.

In her first job after college, she worked on a construction site where male and female workers had to share the portable toilets. Alvarado recalls seeing insulting graffiti about herself in the stalls. It was tough. She considered quitting but liked the work, so she pushed on and soon came up with the idea of starting her own construction company.

As she started bidding on larger projects, an owner turned down one of her proposals, telling her she was too young and inexperienced to handle the job. "Does your mother know you're doing this?" he asked. After that, Alvarado began signing her proposals with just her initials, so that her work would not be prejudged because she was a woman.

Alvarado was respectful, but never shy in trying to break through the "concrete ceiling" in a male-dominated industry, but no one

> **"STRENGTH IS NOT GENDER-BASED. IT IS STANDING TALL FOR WHAT YOU BELIEVE IN, DOING THE RIGHT THINGS, KEEPING FOCUS ON YOUR ABILITY TO SUCCEED, AND BRINGING OTHERS ALONG."**

made it easy. In those years, many banks wouldn't lend money to Latina women. After Alvarado tried to get a loan and was turned down by six banks, her parents mortgaged their home to lend her the money to start her business. (That means her parents took a loan from a bank. If they were unable to repay the loan, then the bank could take their house.) She said that "I paid them back, but I could never repay them for taking that risk."

She created her firm in 1976, when the share of women in construction work was still less than 1 percent. Her first building was a bus shelter. Then came curbs and sidewalks. Next: multimillion-dollar hotels, hospitals, and sports stadiums. But she still had to face down male prejudice.

Even after she became a big shot, many men on construction sites continued to assume she was someone's assistant or girlfriend. An architect who came to her office mistook her for a secretary and told her to check on the coffee. She did so, letting him see how he'd misjudged the situation after the meeting began.

Alvarado broke through another barrier in 1992 when she partnered with six male entrepreneurs as the first woman to bid for a new major league baseball team, the Colorado Rockies. Today, Alvarado is the first Latino (male or female) owner of a professional baseball team.

For decades, Alvarado has worked to help other Latinas climb their own career ladders. In 1998, she was one of the founders of Adelante Mujer, a nonprofit organization designed to help Latina women succeed in higher education and careers.

She always remembers her mother saying, "Empiesa pequeño, pero piensa grande—start small but think big," and learning that, "many of our ideas and perspectives occur during our youth. Open your eyes early on to all the possibilities. But don't just dream about possibilities—take action on your dreams."

Taylor Swift

KNOW YOUR **VALUE**

Anyone working as a musician will tell you the industry is on its deathbed. Anyone, that is, except Taylor Swift. "The music industry is not dying," the singer wrote in a *Wall Street Journal* editorial. "It's just coming alive."

Most musicians would disagree. With so many ways to listen to songs for free, earning a living can be a struggle even for celebrity artists. Yet Swift insists it's possible. "In my opinion, the value of an album is . . . based on the amount of heart and soul an artist has bled into a body of work, and the financial value that artists . . . place on their music when it goes out into the marketplace," she wrote.

Swift knows her value. She knows her fans will pay for her music. *Forbes* ranked her the world's top-paid woman in music in 2016, when she earned $170 million.

You can do it too, Swift maintains. "My hope for the future, not just in the music industry, but in every young girl I meet . . . is that they all realize their worth and ask for it," she wrote.

Swift has not only asked for her worth, she has demanded it. But her value extends beyond her talent as a songwriter, singer, and performer. It's also from being, as *Forbes* business writer Joe Harpaz put it, "on the list of modern-day disruptive business geniuses."

He calls Swift a genius because she realizes it's not enough to be the best at making music. Artists must also build audience platforms, market their music, negotiate contracts, protect their brands, and tirelessly promote themselves and their work.

Swift does all that and more.

In 2014, she decided Spotify was not paying musicians fairly. So she pulled her entire song library from the streaming service. When she was able to negotiate a sweeter agreement in 2017, she put her songs back on.

Swift has figured out strategies to protect her brand and at the same time reward her loyal fans. Usually, when concert tickets go on sale, fans compete with one another and with ticket resellers, or scalpers. Scalpers, who use computer bots to snatch up tickets, hike the prices when they resell them. To outsmart scalpers, Swift came up with an innovative approach. Fans who participate in activities on her website or purchase more of her music and merchandise earn a better chance of buying tickets to her concerts.

Swift began working as a songwriter at 13, when she landed a contract with RCA Records. The following year, she turned down RCA's offer to extend the contract. "I didn't want to be somewhere where they were sure that they kind of wanted me, maybe," she told *Rolling Stone*.

From the beginning, Swift refused to underestimate her worth. It probably helped that her parents worked in finance and could advise her on how to negotiate favorable deals.

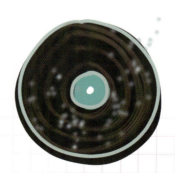

Her parents also helped in other ways. Swift's mother chose a gender-neutral name for Taylor. If she applied for jobs in the male-dominated world of finance, her mother didn't want a potential boss to be able to tell from her resume that she was female.

Nowadays, of course, everyone knows that Taylor is a woman. Millions upon millions of "Swifties" follow her on social media.

Early on, she understood the value of social media. In 2005, while negotiating a contract, she told record-label representatives that she communicated with her fans on "this new site called Myspace." She understood that artists soon would get record deals based on their fan bases, rather than the other way around.

"Music is art, and art is important and rare," Swift wrote in her *Wall Street Journal* editorial. "Important, rare things are valuable. Valuable things should be paid for. It's my opinion that music should not be free, and my prediction is that individual artists and their labels will someday decide what an album's price point is. I hope they don't underestimate themselves or undervalue their art."

Taylor Swift never will. You can bank on it.

> **"THE ONLY REAL RISK IS BEING TOO AFRAID TO TAKE A RISK AT ALL."**

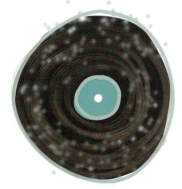

Sheryl Sandberg

GIVE IT ALL YOU'VE GOT

Lean in. If you've heard this phrase, you probably know it's a rallying cry. Its message: Working women should be ambitious and reach for their goals, whatever they may be.

Sheryl Sandberg made the phrase famous with her blockbuster 2013 best-seller, *Lean In: Women, Work, and the Will to Lead*. But long before that, she was following her own good advice.

After earning her BA in economics from Harvard University, where she later returned for a business degree, Sandberg held high-profile jobs for the World Bank, the U.S. Treasury Department, and Google. But she really made her mark after 2008, when Facebook hired her as its chief operating officer. As COO, she reports directly to Facebook CEO Mark Zuckerberg, and she is responsible for day-to-day business affairs. In just 10 years, Sandberg helped turn the 4-year-old company into a $445 billion global powerhouse. She has overseen spectacular growth from about 70 million members to 2 billion members. By 2014, she had become a billionaire and was appearing on lists of the world's most powerful women.

Not everyone has that much natural talent or ambition, of course. Yet on her way to the top, Sandberg came to believe that too many of her female colleagues were holding themselves back. They were "leaning out," as she put it, because of a lack of confidence in

> **"I WOULD CHANGE OUR CULTURE, WHICH TEACHES ALL OF US— WOMEN AND MEN—THAT MEN SHOULD ACHIEVE AND WOMEN SHOULD SUPPORT OTHERS. THE TRUTH IS THAT EVERYONE SHOULD ACHIEVE AND EVERYONE SHOULD SUPPORT OTHERS."**

themselves or worry that they wouldn't be able to be good mothers while holding down a demanding job. According to Sandberg, that meant they were not only limiting their own futures but slowing progress for women in leadership.

In 2010, she gave a TED Talk titled "Why We Have So Few Women Leaders." At the time, less than 5 percent of heads of state and only 13 percent of world parliament members were women, she noted. And in the corporate sector, women filled less than 16 percent of top positions. "The numbers have not moved since 2002 and are going in the wrong direction," Sandberg argued.

Women too often lack confidence and underestimate their achievements, she said. They're less likely than men to take credit for their work. Instead, they'll often say someone helped them, or they got lucky. And this attitude gap matters a lot, Sandberg insists, since women who don't believe in themselves will be less likely to fight for promotions and raises.

The TED Talk hit a nerve. Soon it ignited a global movement. Women forwarded the video to their friends, colleagues, and daughters. Three years later, Sandberg published *Lean In*, selling more than 4 million copies. She announced she would be donating all the profits from the book to a new organization, LeanIn.Org, which would encourage women to aim high in their careers even as they start families. LeanIn.Org has since supported some 36,000 "Lean In Circles" in 162 countries. Lean In Circles are groups of women (and sometimes men too) who meet regularly to share their experiences and learn together. The Lean In website provides downloadable guidelines on how to form a circle and gives advice about topics to discuss, such as how fear of success can hold women back. There are also videos by experts that help teach women how to get better at advocating for themselves. "Your body language and your tone can signal positive emotion!" counsels one of them.

Sandberg notes that one of the biggest obstacles for women trying to get ahead at work is the unfair burden they face at home. Historically, women have done most of the work of running households and raising families. The solution, Sandberg says, is to choose a partner with care. If a woman wants to marry, she should look for someone who won't shirk from washing dishes or changing diapers. Sandberg cites research showing that U.S. married couples who share responsibilities equally and make similar amounts of money are more likely to stay together.

Sandberg has kept up her strong advocacy for women while continuing to help steer Facebook through good times and bad. She sets her sights high, just as she advises her followers to do. She says she won't rest until she reaches the goal of an equal world where "women run half our countries and companies and men run half our homes."

WHO IS TED?

TED—which stands for technology, entertainment, design—is a conference that's been held every year since 1990. At the conference, influential thinkers and leaders in these fields gather and present their ideas (they talk!) in front of a live audience. The TED Talks are also recorded and shared online so that anyone can view them. The most popular TED Talks have been viewed tens of millions of times!

Kimberly Bryant

BE A ROLE MODEL

Kimberly Bryant was accustomed to being the only black woman in the room. She was the only one in her engineering and computer science classes at Vanderbilt University. After graduating in 1989, she was the only one in her office.

Bryant tried to brush aside how lonely she felt seeing no one who looked like her at school or work. But when she dropped off her 11-year-old daughter, Kai, at a coding summer camp, Bryant was stunned by what she saw.

"The class was literally still filled with boys, sprinkled with a handful of girls," she said. "And Kai was the only student of color, boy or girl."

On the drive home after the weeklong sleepaway camp, Kai told Bryant how much she loved designing video games. She also mentioned that the instructors paid more attention to the boys than the girls. Bryant's heart sank. "I had seen this light in her eyes about all she learned. But I didn't want it to get put out prematurely because she didn't get the type of nurturing that she needed," she said. "That was a moment for me to realize I needed to make a change if I wanted to see a change happen in my daughter's world."

Bryant embraced the moment. She began teaching her daughter and some of her friends to code. She wanted to inspire and excite the girls. And she wanted them to experience what she had not—to be surrounded by people who looked like them.

Soon after, Bryant quit her job at a biotechnology company and started a nonprofit called Black Girls Code. Its mission is to change the face of the computing workforce. Women held only 27 percent of technology jobs in the United States in 2017, according to the National Center for Women and Information Technology. The picture was even bleaker for African-American women. They held just 3 percent of the jobs.

Bryant taught the first series of Black Girls Code classes in 2011 in a San Francisco basement. Eight girls came and had to share six computers. At the time, people were just starting to realize how few women and minorities worked in tech. Bryant's timing was right.

After the second six-week course, Google gave the group $20,000—its first grant. Since then, most of the nonprofit's funding has come from corporate grants. In 2017, General Motors gave the organization $225,000 to open a Detroit chapter, its thirteenth.

The organization offers summer camps, weekend workshops, and after-school classes throughout the United States and in South Africa. Students learn basic coding skills and how to design web pages, game apps, and robots.

APPLYING FOR GRANTS

Grants are gifts, usually monetary, from government agencies, foundations (charitable groups), or corporations. Nonprofit organizations such as Black Girls Code often rely on grants for funding so they can provide a service for free or for less than it actually costs. Foundations exist to give away money to worthy causes and people. For many successful companies, charitable giving enhances their image, enabling them to associate their brand with doing good. Nobody throws money at you just because you're doing something cool, though. You have to apply for grants, and the application process can be challenging. You'll have to share a lot of information about your goals and how you plan to use the grant money. But if you've figured out a smart way to make the world a better place, chances are good that you can find funding.

"I love looking around the room and seeing all the girls doing robotics or game design," Bryant said. "That's not something you see every day."

Black Girls Code has connected more than 8,000 girls from underrepresented communities to technology and helped them master the skills necessary to become industry leaders. By 2040, it aims to reach 1 million girls.

One of the fun ways the nonprofit gets girls excited about technology is by sponsoring girls-only hackathons. During a hackathon, computer programmers work together to create new software or solve problems as a group. At one, Kai and her team developed an app to point hungry, homeless people in Oakland, California, to shelters with leftover restaurant food. The group's hackathons have also produced tools to track lost pets and to connect students with mentors. One hackathon team developed an app called "takeAminute," designed to help people relax by matching their behavioral symptoms with YouTube videos intended to calm and amuse them.

"Black Girls Code gives girls not just an opportunity to learn how to code but to use code as a tool for changing the world around them," Bryant said.

She and Black Girls Code are changing the tech world one girl at a time.

> **"YOU HAVE TO HAVE WOMEN AND PEOPLE OF COLOR AT THE TABLE, OR YOU WON'T BE ABLE TO CREATE PRODUCTS THAT REACH AUDIENCES IN A WAY THAT THEY'LL WANT TO USE THEM ON A DAILY BASIS."**

Joy Mangano

TURN NO INTO **YES**

Joy Mangano has spent her life inventing things. While working at an animal hospital as a teenager, she designed a fluorescent flea collar so drivers could see dogs and cats at night and avoid hitting them. A year later, a company called Hartz Mountain introduced a similar pet product. After missing out once, Mangano vowed never to miss another opportunity to market one of her inventions.

In 1989, she found herself divorced, responsible for three children, and struggling financially. She was frustrated that she had to keep replacing her kitchen mop. So she did what came naturally—she invented a better mop. It was cotton so it wouldn't scratch the floor like mops made with synthetic materials. And it had interlocking handles to allow users to wring it out without getting their hands wet or hurting their backs.

She called it the Miracle Mop.

Mangano peddled her self-wringing mop from store to store. Many a door slammed in her face. But she refused to take no for an answer. "When I first showed the buyer for Kmart my Miracle Mop, he told me no," Mangano said. "Not 'maybe' or 'we'll see,' just a flat-out 'no.' 'No, I cannot sell your mop. No one will buy it.'"

Was he ever wrong! But his rejection taught Mangano a lesson that allowed her to go from being a single mother unable to pay her electric bill to being a businesswoman who's sold billions of dollars in products.

Key to her wild success has been her ability to find a way to make a negative into a positive. "I always think: How can I turn this 'no' into a 'yes'? There is always a solution to any problem, and even if it looks like a dead end, it probably isn't," she said.

"Finding your way around the 'no' makes you work harder, be better, and think deeper," she said. "This is a chance to learn something, reset your thinking, and draw motivation—the motivation to prove people wrong."

At times, it was simply a matter of persistence.

In 1992, she pitched her mops to QVC, the cable television shopping network. The network agreed to take 1,000 mops. But when sales lagged, they told Mangano they planned to return the unsold mops. Mangano wouldn't hear of it. She asked the network to allow

REINVENT THE WHEEL

Joy Mangano is always looking for ways to improve existing products. When Mangano found out that 90 percent of luggage is damaged when wheels break off because they stick out, she invented what she called a "spinball" suitcase wheel. It tucks itself in. "You know how people say, 'you don't have to reinvent the wheel?'" she asked. "But I did."

Her Huggable Hangers are covered in a velvety material so clothes do not slip off of them. With one simple change, she solved a common closet problem. The hangers are also extra slim, so they save space in a closet. When she told people she was making velvety hangers, many could not understand why. But a billion hangers later, she's happy to show her doubters how she saw a need and filled it.

her to go on television and sell the Miracle Mop herself. She did, and she sold out. She sold 18,000 mops in 20 minutes.

By 1995, Mangano had sold $1 million worth of Miracle Mops, each priced at $19.95. Today, she's the author of more than 100 patents and trademarks and has sold more than $3 billion in products. Learning to turn a "no" into a "yes" has allowed Mangano to live her American dream.

"EVEN THE SIMPLEST, SMALLEST LITTLE IDEA CAN LITERALLY **CHANGE THE WORLD.**"

Alice Waters

ENVISION, **EMPOWER**, DELEGATE

Alice Waters just wanted to be able to afford to cook for friends when she opened her French restaurant, Chez Panisse, in 1971. But she ended up starting a movement.

She'd visited France, fallen in love with the food, and worked briefly as a teacher. The work left her feeling frustrated. "I'm not patient enough to be a teacher—and that's an understatement!" she wrote in her 2017 memoir, *Coming to My Senses: The Making of a Counterculture Cook*.

She was 27, and her only enjoyment was having friends over for dinner. "I was kind of going broke cooking for them," she wrote. "I thought, 'Hey, if I opened a restaurant, I could keep doing this, but they'd have to pay.'"

That's what happened. Waters designed her restaurant to feel like a warm, well-lit dining room. It offers only one fixed-price menu, which changes daily depending upon the available local fresh fruits, vegetables, cheeses, meats, and fish. Chez Panisse brings the farm to the table.

Not only is the menu different than what you'd find in a typical restaurant, the pricing, the feel of the room, and the entire way Waters has run the business is different. She graduated from the University of California at Berkeley in 1967 with a degree in French cultural studies and a commitment to the ideals of the antiwar and civil rights movements of the 1960s. "We really felt we could change the world," she said. "I still do."

She has. Chez Panisse has influenced the way we eat. It sparked a nationwide push to eat locally, organically, and sustainably. It pioneered a slow-food movement in a fast-food nation.

The restaurant has been a resounding success, operating out of the same brown-shingle house in Berkeley, California, for nearly 50 years. It's still tough to get a reservation. And it still tops lists of the world's best restaurants.

From the beginning, Waters rejected ordinary restaurant organization. She relied instead on her instincts and worked within the anti-establishment culture of Berkeley. At the time, rebellious young people were questioning and challenging everything—from the war in Vietnam to racial inequality to the clothes they wore and the food they ate. "I knew very well that I was running a counterculture restaurant, and that Chez Panisse would never have happened without that movement," she wrote in her memoir. "The idea of having only one menu was preposterous by mainstream standards, and I never could have borrowed money from the banks."

For a while, Waters worked in both the kitchen and the dining room. She boasted that, as a waitress, she could sell anything on the menu, even items that didn't sound particularly appetizing. But she admits she's not as skilled at managing. As a result, the restaurant had some rocky years financially. Waters' parents had mortgaged their house so she could start the business. When hard times hit, her father offered to help. He had taught others how to organize their businesses. He insisted that she buy a computer and hire a business

> **"BECAUSE OF THE COUNTERCULTURE, I COULD RUN MY KITCHEN AS I WANTED, AND DO SO AS A WOMAN. IT WAS PRETTY RARE FOR A WOMAN TO OWN AND RUN A RESTAURANT THEN."**

manager. He came up with an organizational plan and put together a management team. Waters learned to assign tasks to others, or delegate. The fortunes of Chez Panisse turned.

Over the years, she also learned from her father the importance of positive feedback, "to first tell somebody something good about what they're doing, then tell them what they need to do to improve." Waters continues to inspire young chefs in schools and in kitchens around the world and continues to love serving guests at Chez Panisse. Sitting in the restaurant's kitchen on the eve of its 40th anniversary, she said, "There hasn't been one day I didn't want to come here, not one day."

Prerna Gupta

DARE TO BE **DIFFERENT**

As the oldest child of Indian immigrants, Prerna Gupta struggled not to stick out in her small Oklahoma town. In elementary school, when visiting friends complained about the smell of her mother's Indian cooking, she stopped having them over. When her classmates sunbathed at the community pool, she covered her body in towels. The last thing she wanted was for her brown skin to darken. Gupta tried everything she could think of to blend in with the other girls in her all-white suburban neighborhood. But pretending to be like everyone else only made her feel more like an outcast.

By the time she was in high school, she began to warm again to her mother's cooking and her family's cultural traditions. That's when she hit on the key to her success: "Embrace what makes you different. Don't view it as a weakness; view it as a strength." This motto proved essential to her personal happiness and her professional success.

"Having that grit and belief in my own values was so critical to being an entrepreneur," she said. "Everyone tells you as an entrepreneur that your ideas are crazy. Ninety-nine times out of 100 you're going to hear, 'This will never work. What are you doing? This is too risky. Go get a normal job,'" she said.

Gupta created her first business with Parag Chordia, now her husband. They borrowed money from their friends and family to start Yaari, a social-networking site for Indians. It grew to 2 million users. But still, it flopped. By 2008, Facebook dominated the social-networking space and left little room for sites like Yaari.

Gupta and Chordia next focused on their mutual love of music to create Khush, Inc. The company developed Songify, an app that turns speech into music, and LaDiDa, an app that generates background music when you sing a melody. LaDiDa gives everyone a chance to sound like Adele or Beyoncé.

Thanks to Khush, Gupta became a multimillionaire before her 30th birthday. She and Chordia sold the start-up to another company, Smule, for $20 million in 2011.

After the sale, Gupta and Chordia traveled for a year and a half and began writing a young-adult novel together. As they wrote, Gupta wondered how she could pair her knowledge of app development with her love of literature. In 2015, she and Chordia launched Hooked, a mobile app with bite-sized stories that read like text messages.

Much of the money they raised to start Hooked came from stars—people like actor Ashton Kutcher and singer-songwriter Mariah Carey. Usually when entrepreneurs need seed money (money to start businesses), they ask venture capitalists (investors

THE LEAN START-UP

The "lean start-up" is a scientific approach to launching new businesses. Most new businesses start by creating a product they think customers want. They may spend months or years perfecting a product before showing it to the public. In a lean start-up, a company puts out an early version of its product and then gets feedback from customers. The company then tweaks the product and releases a new, better version. It can keep trying until it gets the product right. And, if no one wants to buy the product, the creators will find that out before they've spent a ton of time and money on it.

who provide cash to start companies). But Hooked had the potential for discovering the next hit book, which could become a blockbuster movie. So it appealed to celebrities. By 2018, Hooked had raised $15 million.

In launching Hooked, Gupta and Chordia relied on a scientific approach to creating a product called a lean start-up. It allows CEOs like Gupta to analyze data and adjust their products accordingly. Gupta believes developing a compelling story is a lot like developing a moneymaking tech product. In both cases, it's wise to rely on data. Hooked uses data to guide its decisions about which stories to buy. The company tests the stories on readers to see how far they read. It buys only stories with a completion rate of at least 65 percent.

Hooked also used results from reading tests to hit on its winning formula—breaking up the stories into six-minute segments with the words in text-message chunks. Critics have wondered if Hooked is trying to kill books. On the contrary, Gupta sees her app as a tool to get teens who claim to hate reading "hooked" on it.

Again, she thinks differently. "Young people are spending more and more time staring at the mobile screen," she said. "Why can't we bring fiction to them?" By 2018, Hooked did bring fiction to 40 million readers.

“DATA DOESN'T KILL CREATIVITY. DATA FREES US TO RISK BEING MORE IMAGINATIVE AND TO BE MORE CREATIVE.”

LEARN MORE!

The following books, blogs, and websites may be useful to you if you want to learn more about inspiring, entrepreneurial women—or if you want to start a business of your own!

BOOKS

Better Than a Lemonade Stand! Small Business Ideas for Kids by Daryl Bernstein (Aladdin/Beyond Words, 2012).

How to Start Your Very First Business by the Creators of Warren Buffett's Secret Millionaires Club (Downtown Bookworks, 2015).

How to Turn $100 into $1,000,000 by James McKenna and Jeannine Glista, with Matt Fontaine (Workman Publishing, 2016).

Women in Science by Rachel Ignotofsky (Ten Speed Press, 2016).

BLOGS

kidpreneurs.org/blog

www.quicksprout.com/blog

www.retireat21.com/category/blog#

WEBSITES

blackgirlscode.com

girlswhocode.com

sba.gov/learning-center

teenbusiness.com/girl-bosses

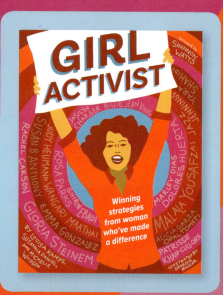

Generation Girl books celebrate amazing women who've been there, done that, and learned some valuable lessons along the way. Be inspired by their stories, learn from their struggles and successes, and get ready to change the world. Look for more hard-won wisdom in: